Contents

Acknowledgements

My thanks go firstly to the children and practitioners who have taught me so much over the years – all very special people.

Thanks, too, go to my editor and friend, Jude Bowen, for her efficient professionalism and unfailing support, which was especially welcome at those times when I wondered whether I could manage.

And last but not least, thanks to Reinhard, especially for doing 'dog duty' on the days when I needed to do nothing but write!

Encouraging Positive Behaviour in the Early Years:

A Practical Guide

Collette Drifte

Paul Chapman Publishing
London · Thousand Oaks · New Delhi

Paul Chapman Publishing
A SAGE Publications Company
1 Oliver's Yard
55 City Road
London EC1Y 1SP

SAGE Publications Inc
2455 Teller Road
Thousand Oaks, California 91320

SAGE Publications India Pvt Ltd
B-42 Panchsheel Enclave
New Delhi 110 017

Library of Congress Control Number 2003115418

A catalogue record for this book is available from the British
Library

ISBN 1-4129-0135-9
ISBN 1-4129-0136-7 (pbk)

Typeset by Pantek Arts Ltd, Maidstone, Kent
Printed in Great Britain by Cromwell Press, Trowbridge, Wiltshire

Biographical details

Collette Drifte is a freelance author and trainer, with 22 years' experience in maintream and special education. A former deputy head teacher and now living in Northumberland, she has written numerous articles and books in the fields of early years special needs and early years literacy. She speaks regularly at national exhibitions and leads courses, workshops and seminars across the country.

For Reinhard, with my love

Introduction

With the introduction of the revised *Special Educational Needs (SEN) Code of Practice* in 2001/2002, the full range of early years care and education was required to plan and implement inclusion. This meant that many settings were included for the first time in far-reaching changes, designed to make sure that early years children who have special needs will, where possible and appropriate, be cared for and educated in a mainstream setting. Providers such as playgroups, registered child-minding networks, pre-school groups, private and non-maintained nurseries and private early years provision were among these settings. As a result, a group of early years practitioners with no experience in working with children who have special needs found themselves in need of training, information and support.

Also, as the policy of inclusion becomes the norm, there appears to be one area of difficulty where early years practitioners really feel they need training, information and support, and this is working with those children whose behaviour causes concern, because it is inappropriate or challenging. If you are trying to support a child with persistently difficult behaviour you may often face a situation where you have to make a quick decision about the best way of dealing with what is happening.

The ever-increasing amount of pressure on practitioners combined with all the other things going on in the setting make it understandable that they may feel deskilled and unsure of what they are supposed to do. It is easy for them to become focused on the negative aspects of the child's behaviour, seeing nothing redeeming in either the child or the situation, and to conclude that there's no solution.

There is a wide range of books and articles on the subject of inappropriate or difficult behaviour, from textbooks giving a full theoretical background of the psychology of the behaviour a child may present, to one-off articles giving some handy hints about what a practitioner could try. You need the time to find these, read them and then decide what would be best for you, and time is a commodity that practitioners do not in have large amounts.

Encouraging Positive Behaviour in the Early Years: A Practical Guide has been written in response to this situation. Many books and articles are written with eye-catching titles such as *Managing Challenging Behaviour* or *Coping with Difficult Behaviour*, which tempt the practitioner to think there's a quick fix to a problem that may be dominating their working day. This book doesn't pretend to do that, because no two children are alike and there's no such thing as a quick fix solution, but it does aim to help the practitioner to stand back from their situation, rethink their own philosophies and practices, review what's going on in the setting and then do something about any element that may need to be changed.

The book speaks of 'inappropriate behaviour', 'unacceptable behaviour' or 'positive behaviour', and never refers to 'a problem child' or 'a difficult child'. This isbecause it isn't the *child* we're hoping to change, but their *behaviour*, and it's very important to keep this aim as the focus of any intervention that is planned. A child's behaviour is influenced by (and indeed may be caused by) many factors such as their home environment, their personal relationships, their past experiences, their personality, their early years setting and its environment, their interaction with the adults in the setting, the practitioners' own experiences, attitudes and behaviour, and a myriad other things that come into play. It's our task as the child's practitioner to identify what factors are influencing the child's behaviour, and to take what steps we can to adjust or adapt these to provide opportunities for the child to develop positive behaviour.

The first chapter of this book explores the concept of inclusion and how it has evolved historically, legally and in practice, with the gradual move from 'integration' to 'inclusion'. It looks in general terms at making sure exclusion does not occur in the early years setting, in relation to children with behavioural difficulties, and it also explores some suggestions that help professionals to develop inclusive practices in the setting's activities.

Chapter 2 asks practitioners some hard-hitting questions about their perceptions of special needs in general, and behavioural difficulties in particular. It shows how practitioners may need to 'peel back' all their beliefs, re-examine their own behaviour and possibly change their attitudes and working practices. It also explores the reasons why and how an early years setting can write a positive behaviour policy, with discussion of and suggestions for the practicalities involved in planning, writing and publishing the policy.

Chapter 3 examines some general principles behind the planning, writing and reviewing of Individual Education Plans (IEPs). It then explores the practicalities involved in writing and reviewing Individual Education Plans specifically for children with behavioural difficulties, including ways of identifying and recording inappropriate behaviour to provide a planning resource. Working with both the child and their family is an important part of this chapter.

The final chapter could be called the 'down to brass tacks' chapter since it addresses the daily realities involved in trying to both reduce undesired and inappropriate behaviour, and to encourage positive behaviour. It looks at the theory behind the psychology-based *ABC approach* to working with children who have behavioural difficulties and actually putting the *ABC approach* into practice, with practical suggestions for avoiding, managing and reducing inappropriate behaviour, and for encouraging desired behaviour.

Throughout the book there are useful photocopiable forms, together with completed examples alongside each one. These forms can be used as they stand, or adapted for a specific setting. There is also a sample positive behaviour policy that practitioners may like to use as a framework for their own, again to be adapted if required, to better suit a particular setting, or to use as it stands.

There are case studies running through the book to highlight specific points where appropriate, all of which feature real children in real situations. To protect the children's identities, their names have been changed. Occasionally I use a non-existent child called Buster to highlight a discussion point in the text. While the child doesn't exist, Buster does – he's a persona doll I have used successfully with children who were experiencing behavioural difficulties – and I decided to use his name rather than strive for political correctness by using a variety of names, and possibly still end up unintentionally offending somebody.

Finally, there is a Further Reading list for those practitioners who would like more information, suggestions and support about behavioural difficulties. The books recommended have all been chosen because they are 'reader-friendly' and also very practical. Practitioners may not have either the time or the inclination to plough through heavy, academic texts, and the listed titles are certainly not of this genre.

JUST FOR FUN

The education field, like many other professional areas, is full of acronyms that can leave us with eyes rolling around in our heads. You might like to try completing the crossword overleaf without cheating, and see how many acronyms connected with special educational needs or early years you know. If you're really stuck, you can check in the Glossary, or even look at the solution, both at the end of the book. Good luck!

Acronym crossword puzzle

Across

1 A partnership for the development and care of early years children
4 A support service for learning
6 A short educational psychologist?
8 The setting's named special needs person
10 An action programme for one
11 Learning by speaking, listening and working all together with ICT etc
13 A support service for children who have visual or hearing difficulties
14 A short play plan?
15 One's plan to actually *do* something

Down

1 Challenging behaviour?
2 A support service for parents
3 The current government department in charge of education
5 Reduce special educational needs
7 Somebody allocated to help a child to learn
9 The service of 6 across
10 A tailor-made plan for one child's education
12 A regional department in charge of education

Chapter 1

How to make sure your setting is fully inclusive

(or: All Together Now 123)

In this chapter we will explore the concept of inclusion by:

- discussing how it has evolved historically, legally and in practice;

- looking at an overview of legislative developments from 1978 to 2002;

- tracking the gradual move from 'integration' to 'inclusion';

- discussing ways to ensure exclusion does not occur;

- exploring ways of developing inclusive practices in the setting's activities, in relation to children with behavioural difficulties.

You may well wonder what relevance education laws have to your setting and why you shouldn't ignore them and, apart from making sure you have regard to the *Special Educational Needs Code of Practice*, just get on with the job of working with your children in an inclusive and welcoming way. But in order to make sure that your setting is indeed inclusive, you need to be aware of how the concept of inclusion developed and became the accepted way of working that it should be today. While the legislation is in place to ensure inclusion, as professionals we need to be vigilant that we really are practising inclusion in our settings. This is not because the law requires it (although it does), but because every child, regardless of their difficulties, has the right to have their abilities and achievements celebrated, and to be helped to fulfil their potential, in a setting that sees them in a positive light. Only by having a truly inclusive setting will this happen.

The legislative developments since 1978 show how we have moved towards today's position of having inclusive settings as the norm, and we need to have an understanding of those developments to ensure the best inclusive provision possible for the children in our care.

AN OVERVIEW OF SEN LEGISLATION

Before 1978, children who had 'problems' were put into segregated schools, institutions or hospitals, usually according to a disability or difficulty, as perceived by those in authority. Very often these children were labelled with names we would not tolerate today such as 'mentally handicapped', 'crippled', 'spastic' or, in the case of children with behavioural difficulties, 'maladjusted'. The *Warnock Report* was published in 1978 and led to the 1981 Education Act, the first major legislation which recognised that a child's difficulties are interactive and contextual, in other words not within the child or needing 'treatment'. This Act made us rethink our way of working with children who have special educational needs, often needing a complete turnabout from established practices that we thought were tried and true. We realised that we had to take a long, hard look at ourselves, whether we were failing to meet a child's needs, and if so, how. The term 'integration' was coined and local education authorities (LEAs) were keen to show their commitment to the idea. There were many schemes put into place, such as attaching special needs units to mainstream schools, or having special needs classes within schools, and integrating the children at certain times of the day or week.

In 1989 the Children Act was passed, requiring identification of and provision for disabled children, particularly those under 8 years of age. This Act was also very important because for the first time, disabled children were included in the wider framework of legal powers, duties and protections relating to all children.

Then the 1981 Act was repealed with the 1993 Education Act which maintained and strengthened the principles at the heart of the 1981 legislation. It continued the child's entitlements and there was more focus on both the involvement and empowerment of the child's parents, particularly through the establishment of an SEN tribunal to give them the right of appeal.

In 1994, the first *SEN Code of Practice* was put into place and provided guidelines for implementing the 1993 Act. The *Code of Practice* established a standardised framework for the provision of appropriate and individualised education for children with special needs. This meant that wherever a child lived or moved to, the provision should be seamless and continuous. The reality was, of course, a little different. Depending on the LEA's resources, children were given varying degrees of support and allocation of resources. For example, some authorities would give a Learning Support Assistant to a specific child while others would say that the child should be taught in group or class situations with the LSA.

The Disability Discrimination Act was passed in 1995 and clarified the rights of employment, obtaining services and goods, buying or renting land or property, and transport of people with disabilities. Under this Act, somebody is deemed to be 'disabled' if they have a physical or mental impairment that has a substantial and long-term adverse effect on their ability to carry out normal daily activities. Education, including most early years settings, was not covered under this Act, except as providers of goods and services, and was covered only when the 2001

Special Educational Needs and Disability Act was passed (see below). From 1996, the social (but not educational) care of children in private, voluntary and statutory early years settings that were not classed as schools, was covered under this 1995 Act.

From 1996, the Nursery Education and Grant Maintained Schools Act required all early years providers to 'have due regard' to the *SEN Code of Practice*. Children in the care of nursery schools and other maintained settings who had special educational needs were entitled to appropriate provision and their parents were granted greater rights. The duties of schools were made more specific and the regulations for assessing children and issuing Statements of Special Educational Needs were tightened up, for example by setting time limits for the process to be completed.

The 1997 Green Paper *Excellence for All Children* was followed by the*1998 SEN Action Plan* with its strong emphasis on inclusion, parent partnership and multi-agency collaboration. By this time, the term 'integration' was commonly used, but the idea of 'inclusion' was becoming more common. The *SEN Action Plan* emphasised the importance of the holistic approach, acknowledging that positive working practices meant working in partnership with parents and other agencies.

The 2001 Special Educational Needs and Disability Act amended the 1995 Disability Discrimination Act by covering the educational provision that had been excluded. This Act updated and strengthened the *SEN Code of Practice* and strongly emphasised inclusion. For the first time *all* early years providers, including playgroups, registered childminding networks, pre-school groups, out-of-school clubs and so on, had a duty not to discriminate against a disabled child in their provision of education and day care or other services, on the grounds of the child's disability. They had an obligation to implement the *SEN Code of Practice*, making sure their setting is fully inclusive.

The definitions of special educational needs in the *SEN Code of Practice* include children with emotional or behavioural difficulties, so it is clear that these children have as equal an entitlement to positive, inclusive provision as any other. But it is extremely important to remember that we shouldn't be offering inclusive provision because it's a legal requirement, but because we care enough about the children we work with to want the best for them. Part of the best is making sure they have the same chances as everybody else in their group to fulfil their potential in a positive and warm environment.

So, in the context of an early years setting, you have to make reasonable adjustments to ensure you aren't discriminating against children with a disability, and this includes children who have behavioural difficulties. In practical terms, this means that you must not:

- refuse a service;

- offer a worse standard of service; or

- offer a service on worse terms

unless you can give a 'justification' for doing so. 'Justification' for offering different ('worse') circumstances for working with the child means that you can consider:

- Health and Safety issues;

- the needs of the child;

- resources;

- practicality and the interests of the other people in the setting.

The language of the *SEN Code of Practice* is couched in educational terms, referring to 'schools' and 'pupils', but this doesn't mean that other early years settings are not included. The *Code* makes the point that, despite this, its provisions are for *all* early years settings, including for the first time those we have already discussed above.

2001 SPECIAL EDUCATIONAL NEEDS AND DISABILITY ACT

Let's look at parts of the 2001 Act, as it relates to early years settings, in a little more detail, bearing in mind that children with behavioural difficulties are deemed to be children who have special educational needs.

Part I of the 2001 Act amended Part IV of the 1996 Education Act and, among other things:

- changed the conditions that limited the LEA's duty to provide a mainstream place for a child with special educational needs – so LEAs must try as far as possible to place a child with their peers in a mainstream setting;

- required settings to inform parents when they make special education provision because they have identified a child as having special educational needs – so parents must be told by a setting when the practitioners have concerns about a child and begin to differentiate the child's curriculum;

- allowed settings to request a statutory assessment in the same way that parents can – so widening the opportunities for a child's needs to be identified and met;

- required LEAs to provide and advertise parent partnership services – so giving parents more support and advice if they want it;

- required LEAs to make arrangements for resolving disagreements between parents and schools and between parents and the LEA – so making sure that parents can have their problems solved amicably and fairly, which can only be to the benefit of the child;

- tightened up arrangements for appeals to the SEN Tribunal, including setting time limits for the implementation of the Tribunal's decisions – so making sure that issues are not allowed to drag on for great lengths of time before being resolved.

Part II of the 2001 Act amended the 1995 Disability Discrimination Act and:

- made it unlawful to discriminate against disabled children or prospective children;

- set out a duty on settings not to treat disabled children less favourably than non-disabled children;

- required settings to make reasonable adjustments to ensure that they do not put disabled children at a substantial disadvantage.

Each of these clauses shows how settings must do everything to make sure the children aren't excluded from activities on the grounds of their difficulties (remembering that children with behavioural difficulties are included here).[1]

INCLUSION OR INTEGRATION – ARE THEY THE SAME THING?

The simple answer to our question is 'no'. Even now, the two terms tend to be used interchangeably, but they mean very different things and practitioners need to understand the differences, and use each term in the correct context.

Integration

This concept was at the heart of the early provision for children with special educational needs, following the 1981 Education Act. It was based on the **medical model** of the child and their difficulties, which were perceived as coming from within the child, and needing remediation or treatment. (Do you remember the 'remedial reading teacher' in your own school as a child?) When the child with special needs was integrated, they were placed in a mainstream setting and expected to change and adapt in order to 'fit in'. The idea didn't encourage or make possible any changes in attitude that may have been necessary within the setting, whether of its practices or its personnel, for the child to participate as fully as possible. In other words, *the onus was on the child to change.*

Inclusion

This concept has been at the heart of working practices since about 1996 and is based on the **social model** of the child where their difficulties are viewed holistically, and ways of supporting them are found by exploring every aspect of the child's situation. When the child is placed in a mainstream setting, it's the setting that has to change and adapt in order to make sure the child is able to participate as fully as possible. If necessary, the practitioners within the setting must review their attitudes, policies and practices to ensure that it is a fully inclusive organisation. In other words, *the onus is on the setting and everybody involved in it to change.* (For a more detailed discussion of how you can change attitudes, policies and practices, see Chapter 2, Can you stand up to self-scrutiny?, page 23.)

Can you tell which is which?

Have a look at these scenarios and decide whether the practice reflects the medical or social model. (You will find the answers on page 17.)

1 **Jason** finds it hard to wait for his turn to play with a toy and usually snatches it away from the child who's playing with it. Each time this happens, Jenny, his practitioner, takes the toy from him, telling him to leave the play area and that until he learns to play properly he won't be allowed there again.

2 **Annan** has difficulty with sessions in the Large Hall and usually runs around screaming and jostling the other children. His practitioners have rescheduled the sessions to take place when the student nursery nurse is with them and she stays with Annan to support him. If he begins to behave inappropriately, the student takes him aside to share a story until he settles again and can rejoin the other children.

3 **Ned**'s setting follows the Foundation stage curriculum and takes the early learning goals very seriously. He's still working at the stepping stones level, mainly because the area of personal, emotional and social development is where he's having difficulties. His maths abilities are very good but the practitioners in the setting feel he should be following the curriculum at the same level across all areas.

4 At 'Let's Talk' time, **Minnie** isn't asked to make a contribution to group discussions because Lily, her practitioner, knows that she will disrupt the session. There isn't any point in depriving the other children of a good discussion, so Minnie can just listen. Because Minnie doesn't join in, her ability level in this area of learning is difficult to gauge.

5 **Hugh** sometimes behaves inappropriately when he's out with his group at the shops or in the park. One of his practitioners, Margery, feels he should be left at the setting because he's a danger and takes too much of her time and attention from the other children. Pauline, Hugh's other practitioner, rearranges the weekly outing to happen first thing in the morning, and persuades Hugh's grandma, who drops him off each day, to join the group and support Hugh while they're all out on the trip.

DOES INCLUSION HAVE ANY ADVANTAGES?

By taking time to plan an inclusive setting, practitioners will enable both the adults and the children to benefit from the many positive outcomes that good practice will generate. Let's have a look at a few of these.

● *Children benefit from contact with all their peers, regardless of their difficulties.* The practitioner who lovingly encourages a child with behavioural difficulties to develop positive and appropriate behaviour will be an excellent role model for the other children. They will also interact with that child in a positive way, and this in turn will influence the way the child interacts with the others in their group.

- *Practitioners and other adults involved with the setting benefit from contact with children who have special educational needs.* The example of the practitioners' positive attitude towards the child with behavioural difficulties can influence the way other adults involved with the setting interact with the child. Getting to know the real (and likeable) child behind the inappropriate behaviour can correct many myths and misperceptions held by the adults.

- *Parents are more likely to choose mainstream primary schools for their children if they and their children have experienced positive and inclusive pre-school practices.* If practitioners perceive that it's the child's behaviour that is the difficulty and not the child, they can work together with the parents to plan effective strategies for encouraging positive behaviour. This is likely to lead to the parents opting to continue sending their child to mainstream provision later on.

- *Good practice in the care and education of children with special educational needs can improve good practice for **all** the children in the setting.* Almost like a ripple effect, when practitioners plan strategies that are inherently good practice in working with the child who has behavioural difficulties, they will automatically plan positive and effective strategies for all the children's needs and abilities.[2]

SO HOW DO WE 'DO' INCLUSION?

Now we've looked at the theory, let's explore some practical aspects of inclusion and what it means for early years practitioners in relation to children with behavioural difficulties. Your setting will be inclusive if you:

- ensure that all the children work together, regardless of their difficulties, including behavioural difficulties;

- arrange for the child with behavioural difficulties to have support from specialists (for example the LEA's Behaviour Support Service or an educational psychologist) if this is thought to be necessary;

- have changed the setting's attitudes, practices and policies to ensure, where possible, the inclusion of all children, regardless of their difficulties (See Chapter 2 for a more detailed discussion of this aspect of inclusion);

- focus on the child's strengths and abilities when planning an appropriate and supportive curriculum for them (see Chapter 3 for a more detailed discussion of planning IEPs);

- accept difference as ordinary; in other words not to judge the child on their behaviour if it is different from that of their peers, and then view the child in a negative light as a result;

- ask for the views of the child with behavioural difficulties (where you can) and act upon them; this will go a long way to making the child feel cared for, involved and supported, and their appropriate behaviour will gradually develop as a result.

QUIZ TIME

Are the following scenarios examples of inclusive practice? If not, what strategies might the practitioners use to make sure the child is included? (Answers on page 18.)

1   **Marco**, who is almost 4, has been diagnosed as having Attention Deficit Hyperactive Disorder (ADHD) and he takes the drug Ritalin. He goes to his local pre-school group and when he arrives, he tends to run wildly around the room crashing into the furniture and the other children. Some of the parents have complained and the practitioners have asked Marco's parents to withdraw him from the group.

2   **Sophie**, who is 3, goes to nursery every day and is dropped off very early by her mother on the way to work. Most afternoons, Sophie will move between activity areas pushing the other children or spoiling their games or work, usually ending up in tears. The practitioners discussed the problem with Sophie's Mum and decided to let Sophie have a nap after lunch while the other children have Quiet Time, so that she's refreshed for the afternoon's activities.

3   **Pollyanna** is 4 and goes to playschool. She finds difficulty in working in large groups such as story time or discussions, usually disrupting the session with inappropriate behaviour. One of the practitioners takes Pollyanna for a one-to-one session in the library while the others have the group session so ensuring the other children's activity isn't ruined.

4   **Danny**, who is 3, always made a mess at snack time in his nursery, by taking biscuits off the plate and throwing them on the floor, and by tipping his beaker of juice all over the table. The practitioners decided to give him a drinking cup with a sealed lid. They also changed the system with the biscuits, by giving each child a turn (including Danny) at distributing them to the others.

HOW CAN WE AVOID EXCLUSIVE PRACTICES?

There isn't a simple answer to this, because each situation has to be looked at in its own right. Settings, staff, children and circumstances are all unique and need their tailor-made approaches. It's easy when you're in a busy early years setting to make decisions and plans concerning a child that inadvertently exclude them. You may decide something in good faith, genuinely believing it to be for the best all round, but on closer scrutiny it might really be depriving the child of a valuable opportunity or experience. You have to be ruthless with yourself and ask whether your decision is for yourself or for the child. There will be times when your professional judgement is justified and a decision really is in the child's interests, as long as everybody else on the team agrees and supports your reasons. But as a rule-of-thumb, always ask yourself, 'Is this decision really for Buster's development, or for my convenience?'

Here are a few examples of exclusion, all of them real scenarios, although the children's names have been changed.

1   **Sadie's** nursery class is attached to the local primary school and the children always join in the annual Sports Day. This is organised by Mr Davies, the teacher in charge of PE in the school. He knows that Sadie has behavioural difficulties because he's heard her practitioners discussing her in the staff room. He has also dealt with several incidents of Sadie's inappropriate behaviour when he was on duty in the yard at playtime. He has told Sadie's practitioners that he's not prepared to take responsibility for either Sadie's safety or that of the other children if they're involved with Sadie in any incident on Sports Day. They all discuss the situation and decide that Sadie should stay at home on that day, to avoid any accidents and/or clashes with Mr Davies.

2   **Ben's** pre-school group has arranged to go to the zoo for their summer trip. Ben has behavioural difficulties and, in situations where he feels unsure of himself, is inclined to run around wildly and scream. He's been known to run through the yard gates onto the street. The group has just enough adults to go with the children on the trip, but the practitioners feel that Ben needs one-to-one supervision. His Mum has offered to go, but the practitioners refused on the grounds that mothers weren't allowed, so they couldn't make an exception for one and not any of the others. It was decided to tell Ben's Mum that they preferred Ben not to join the trip.

3   **Emma's** nursery has been rehearsing the Nativity Play for several weeks, and she has been given the part of an angel, because for this role she doesn't have to say any lines. Emma's behavioural difficulty means that she finds it hard to stay still for more than a few minutes and unfortunately the part of an angel requires her to stay almost motionless for most of the play. During rehearsals Emma has been very fidgety and as the big day draws nearer, she becomes extremely disruptive. The practitioners decide that Emma shouldn't be in the play because they fear that her behaviour will ruin it, which wouldn't be fair to all the other children who have worked so hard during rehearsals. Emma's Mum is told that Emma can stay with her in the audience on the day of the real performance.

In each of these instances, the practitioners offered reasons for their decisions that they felt were justifiable. You may agree with them and feel that you would have done the same had you been in their position. But in each case, the reality is that the exclusion of the child from the activity meant less pressure for the practitioner to supervise the child, when they had the others to attend to, as well as the activity itself. In each case, the practitioners' decision meant that the child was deprived of the activity and the experiences it offered. Whose convenience was being considered?

HOW CAN WE DEVELOP INCLUSIVE PRACTICES?

You'll have to decide on *general* strategies for ensuring inclusion in your setting when you plan your positive behaviour policy (see Chapter 2). But you won't be able to make specific plans and arrangements for any particular child until you're working with them and know what makes them tick. As we have already discussed, each case is unique, and ways of promoting inclusion for a specific child have to be appropriate, effective for and relevant to that child. What works for one child may be ineffectual for another.

There are some general principles you can adopt, however, which will go some way to helping you to put the theory into practice.

- Ask the parents or carers whether the child's behavioural difficulties occur at home as well. They are the experts in their child and know better than anybody how the child reacts to things. If you forge a positive and cooperative relationship with them, they should feel comfortable to share information with you. Always remember to respect their confidentiality (except in cases where you may suspect abuse of some kind). The difficulties being experienced by the child may be short-term and the parents may be able to explain the cause. If, on the other hand, the difficulties seem to be deeper-rooted and potentially longer-term, working with the parents is crucial for planning a positive way forward.

- Decide together as a staff and with the child's parents what will be the most effective strategies for dealing with their inappropriate and/or unacceptable behaviour. (You will find a more detailed discussion of this in Chapter 2, page 31.) Again, the information about the child that the parents can share with you will often give you a clue as to what will work for them.

- Find out whether anything specific triggers an outburst of inappropriate behaviour in the child. If you can put your finger on something, take action to avoid or prevent the child being placed in that position. (Chapter 3, page 48 discusses this point as does Chapter 4, page 74.)

- If the child has Attention Deficit Disorder (ADD) or Attention Deficit Hyperactive Disorder (ADHD), ask for advice. The child's parents must be the first source of information and if you feel you'd like more specialised advice from a medical professional, always ask the parents' permission before approaching outside agents. You can also exploit the many good, readable books that are available, and there are many websites where you can obtain advice, support and information. Just type 'Attention Deficit Disorder' into your search engine.

- Give the physically aggressive child plenty of learning activities. By having available a lot of games, activities and things to do, the child has fewer opportunities to be hanging around with nothing to do and become bored. This can easily happen if your attention is on another child for the moment, and the child's way of filling unoccupied time is to behave inappropriately. Try to make sure every bit of 'dead time' can be used positively and effectively. (NB

– avoid setting the child senseless tasks such as colouring in or completing photocopiable sheets. These will mean nothing to them, particularly if they're expected to do the task on their own. Give them something practical, meaningful and with something positive to show for it on completion.)

- Never accept aggressive behaviour and always reward positive behaviour. While you can't be continually chastising the child and have to let some things go, it's very important to let them know that you won't tolerate aggression under any circumstances. How you go about this will depend on the child – a sanction that works with one child will be meaningless to another – but you must get that message across. The flip side of that coin is watching for any positive behaviour by the child and immediately praising them for it, making them feel good about what they've done.

- Establish a few essential ground rules to be followed consistently by everyone. These should be simple, meaningful, positive and consistently followed by *everybody*, adults as well as children. (See Chapter 2, page 28 for a more detailed discussion.)

- If appropriate, withdraw the child from group situations for a while and encourage them to talk through their feelings with an adult. There may be a good reason why the child finds it difficult to cope in a group situation, and you may not be aware of it. By encouraging the child to talk to a trusted adult, you may find the key to unlocking some of the child's problems in this regard.

- Watch for and support the introverted and withdrawn child. It's very easy in the hubbub of an early years setting to miss the child that's 'good' and 'quiet'. We all know about the disruptive child who makes their presence felt from Day One, but the child who doesn't command our attention because they're not loud may also have behavioural or emotional difficulties. I'm not talking about the shy child who may be temporarily overwhelmed by the buzz of activity, but about the child who is seriously a loner and continues to be when it's time they had settled and come out of their shell.

- For the child who finds groups hard to handle, work with them initially in a one-to-one situation using fun activities. As their confidence and positive behaviour increase, so you can make the size of the working group larger by gradually introducing more children, one at a time.

- Support the child in whole-class/group sessions. When you feel they're ready to work in the full group, be there to support them at first until they seem to be able to handle the situation with confidence. 'Support' may be anything from having the child close to you, in reach of a gentle and reassuring touch, to allocating an adult to guide the child through the sessions until they're ready to 'fly solo'. Knowing the child well will give you an indication of the best way of planning the support.

- Be ready with a fun activity when the child arrives at the start of the session. Drop-off time is hectic in the most organized of settings and while your back is turned, the child may end up in a situation where their behaviour is inappropriate. By having something exciting and meaningful for the child to do straight away, you may well be avoiding any difficult moments.

- Keep to the daily routine as much as possible. Children with behavioural difficulties need consistency and stability. Sometimes they're totally thrown by changes in routine or unexpected alterations, and the only way they can handle it is with inappropriate behaviour. It's important that you keep the 'staple' activities as regular as possible. If there are going to be some changes to the day's routine, warn the child beforehand, using something concrete to show them, such as an egg-timer or an alarm clock – 'When the alarm rings on the clock, it'll be time to tidy up the painting things and go for our rehearsal for the Christmas play.'

THE CHILD AND INCLUSION

We can easily become fixated on making sure the child is included by differentiating their curriculum and planning IEPs, without realising that inclusion goes further than that. Inclusion almost has to be in the air supply of the setting – automatically absorbed and carried out by everybody in everything they do. Even simple interactions and exchanges should be inclusive. 'Everybody's lining up beautifully except you, Buster' is less likely to stimulate Buster to line up appropriately than 'Right, everybody, line up beautifully, just like Suzanne – well done Suzanne. That's it, Buster, I can see you're trying hard at lining up as well; good boy!' Even if Buster isn't lining up beautifully at that point, by including him in the general praise, he will eventually be encouraged to copy the others. Peer example is a wonderful resource you can exploit to the full.

As practitioners, we also need to make sure that every member of the group and their contribution to the day's activities are valued. They may not have made achievements at the same level as some of the other children, but remember we're measuring them against themselves, and if something they've achieved is a step forward *for them*, we must openly acknowledge it and give them due credit. Public praise reinforces the child's achievements and motivates them to try the next challenge. Be aware though, that the child with behavioural difficulties may find it difficult to handle praise or positive comments at first because they could be so used to being told off. It's possible that when you start to praise their efforts at positive behaviour, they'll react negatively, but treat the child sensitively, and keep praising them. In time, they'll be able to take public praise in their stride.

It's important that the child's opinions are heard and respected by everybody else. Even if it goes against that of the majority, you should acknowledge its validity and respect it. By dismissing or rejecting the child's opinion, a signal is being sent out that what they've said has no value. For a child whose self-esteem may already be at an all-time low, this can be shattering. And it's guaranteed that the child won't try to make a contribution to the next discussion. You need to develop an atmosphere where the child is comfortable enough to speak out, knowing they won't be ridiculed or turned away.

WHAT ELSE CAN I DO?

Here are a few ideas.

- Use your baseline assessments or the Foundation stage profile to check the child's achievement level in the area of personal, emotional and social development and plan their next targets from that point.

- Involve the child's parents and, whenever you can, the child as well in planning their Individual Education Plan (IEP). The information they can supply about the child can be pooled with your existing knowledge to make sure that the IEP you plan is appropriate, achievable and effective. (For a more detailed discussion about planning effective IEPs for children with behavioural difficulties, see Chapter 3.)

- Observe the child at work and play. Find out what motivates, stimulates, excites and challenges them. You can use this information to plan the rewards and sanctions that form an integral part of their IEP. (For a more detailed discussion about rewards and sanctions, see Chapter 4, page 72.)

- When the child has behaved in a positive and desirable way, even if it was for a fleeting moment and even if it wasn't the final target of their IEP, give them lots of praise and some form of reward – something that has meaning for the child – to motivate them to continue trying, and to show them exactly what it is you're expecting of them with regard to their behaviour.

- Involve the children in their own record keeping. They are usually really excited when they see their achievement charts growing or their merit stickers filling up a folder. Or they may get a buzz out of keeping a log of all the extra computer sessions they 'earned'. Knowing your child will tell you what form of record keeping will be best for them, but the important thing is to actively involve them.

- If the child has communication difficulties, it's worthwhile taking the time to learn a signing system such as Makaton, which has symbols as well as text. Many children with special educational needs find this system helpful and the other children in the setting quickly pick it up, becoming enthusiastic users too. You can liaise with your local speech and language therapy department to find out how to access a training course.

- If the child seems to be distressed on admission to your setting, it often helps if you allow them to bring a 'comfort blanket' or favourite toy from home until they settle. You need to be alert though that it goes home at the end of the child's session, or there will be a distressed little person at home for the rest of the day and evening!

- Try to allocate a key worker to the child. This doesn't mean nominate somebody to work on a one-to-one basis all the time with the child, unless of course this has been recommended and you have the resources. It means deciding on an adult in the setting who has made a trusting relationship with the child and encouraging the child to go to that person whenever they feel in need of support, or want to talk. Realistically, of course, this isn't always possible. It depends on how well staffed and resourced your setting is, but if you can manage to do it, the child will benefit.

- Always speak to the child in a positive way. This might sound facile and obvious, but it's surprising how often we speak to children using negative language without realising it. Take a moment to think of your own use of language to the children. How often do you say things like 'Don't run around indoors', 'You mustn't say rude words like that' or 'You can't use my pen'? Turned around, these phrases have a positive equivalent that is much more acceptable: 'Walk around the room, please', 'Try to use polite words like "Go away" rather than those words' and 'Use the big felt tips from the art area instead of my pens'. Simple as it may seem, practices like these all contribute to creating a positive and pleasant atmosphere for everybody, not least the children with behavioural difficulties, who often seem to hear nothing but 'don'ts' all the time.

- Make sure you face the child when speaking and don't turn away until you've finished speaking. Some children have difficulties keeping in their head what you've said to them, once you lose eye contact and break the link between you. If they're not linked into you, their concentration may wander and they'll start to do other things, such as poking Mary beside them, or picking at the loose thread in the carpet, so losing everything you're saying to them, even when it's exciting. Keep bringing your eyes back to Buster and maintain that contact with him.

- Make sure your facial expression is always relaxed and warm. Children can be very good at reading body language and non-verbal gestures. If they've experienced lots of adults continually being cross with them, they probably know little else than frowns and tight lips. Try to overcome this by keeping a smile and twinkling eyes for the child, even if you have to pretend at times. It's all part of the building up of trust and closeness.

- Watch for any personality clashes and change the routine to avoid difficult situations, if necessary. There could be relationship difficulties between the child and other children, or between the child and an adult in the setting. Disharmony has no place in an inclusive setting and you should do all you can to reduce it. (For more discussion about this, see Chapter 2, page 24.)

- If the child has any equipment, communication systems or other special facilities to support them, take the time to learn how to use them properly. Again, to build up trust and a positive relationship with the child, you need good communication.

THE SETTING AND INCLUSION

While establishing positive relationships within the setting is crucial for including the child with behavioural difficulties, so too is providing an environment that is safe, warm, welcoming and with appropriate resources for both supporting and including the child. Try to see your working areas from the point of view of a child with behavioural difficulties. They may find things that are confusing, overwhelming, too challenging, too easy, lacking in excitement or stimulation or even boring. Any of these could be the cause of the child behaving inappropriately.

- Have a look at the physical layout of your room(s) and change it around if necessary to enable the children with behavioural difficulties to access the resources and equipment. Display pictures, labels and captions at a child-friendly height. Frustration at not being able to see pictures properly or take out equipment easily could result in some undesirable behaviour.

- Reassess the furniture, making sure that chairs and tables are the right height for comfortable working. You may think this sounds bizarre, but if the child is uncomfortable they will soon begin to lose concentration, to fidget about and eventually end up in bother. If they're spending quite a bit of their time in discomfort, it's hardly surprising if they become tetchy with the people around them.

- Make sure there is space between pieces of furniture. If the child is prone to be a bit 'physically extrovert', they're less likely to hurt themselves if there is plenty of room between tables and cupboards.

- Make sure the floor is not polished, to give a more secure foothold. If the child tends to zoom around when they're behaving inappropriately, they'll be less likely to slip. Also keep the floor clear of small items such as pencils or Lego, for the same reason.

- Keep furniture and designated areas in the same place and keep the layout of apparatus the same, especially if it's used in another room or hall. Most children with behavioural difficulties need stability and consistency of routine, and this can include the physical aspects of the setting. If you change things around, some children simply can't handle the disruption, and the only way they know of responding is to behave inappropriately. If you do need to have a change around, prepare the child beforehand, warning them what's going to happen and even involving them by encouraging them to give you a hand. Do this with safety in mind, though, making sure any jobs you give them are simple and appropriate.

- Reduce the likelihood of confusion about the day's routine and activities by having your timetable or timeline in symbolic or pictorial form, as well as written. If the child's literacy skills are at a level that prevents them from reading your timetable, they need to be able to interpret it another way, and pictures or symbols are ideal for this. (See Chapter 4, page 80 for more about pictorial timelines and timetables.)

● Choose books that are appropriate for the children in terms of age, interests and achievement level. Select literature that appeals to the children, that interests and excites them, and makes them want to read the book over and over again. This is where knowing the child comes in handy. If they have a deep interest in dinosaurs, make sure you have books about dinosaurs as well as all the other topics you'd like them to discover. Make the books available to everybody and use them together, regularly. Buying the books and displaying them attractively isn't the end of your job. You need to share the books with the children, read them to the little ones, put on funny voices, encourage the children to join in where there are refrains or obvious phrases. When you've introduced a book to the children, leave it out for them to explore in their own time. You'll probably hear them 'reading' it aloud, using *your* intonation and expression! Then share it again with them at another time.

● Always have a quiet area available where the child can go for pleasant 'time out' and to relax a little. (See Chapter 4, page 82.)

● Some children with behavioural difficulties find it very hard to put their feelings into words; others find it hard to acknowledge that they have difficulties behaving appropriately. Using persona dolls or puppets to help the child explore their feelings can be a positive form of support. You can project the difficulties being experienced by the child onto the persona doll in a bid to help them identify with the character and begin to work through their difficulties. For example, you could say, 'Buster, this is Pedro. He sometimes gets really angry when somebody else has got the toy he wants and so he hits them and snatches the toy. He'd like to be able to ask for the toy politely so can you help him to think of a way to do this?' (For more details about persona dolls, see the note at the end of the chapter.)

● Use dolls or puppets as part of story time, circle time or group discussions to support the child who has difficulties managing themselves in this kind of situation. As we have just discussed, the child may be able to contribute to the session by talking through the doll or puppet and projecting themselves this way.

As we come to the end of this chapter, you might like to ask yourself the following questions:

1 Do I know the difference between *integration* and *inclusion*?

2 Does the legislation, both past and present, make sense to me in terms of the development of the philosophy of inclusion and how it is practised today?

3 Do I need to review my setting in terms of its inclusive practice? If so, does the whole setting need to be revised or just some aspects of my work?

4 Do I make sure that none of my children is inadvertently excluded from any activities on offer?

5 Am I truly putting inclusive practices into place in my work?

SUMMARY

In this chapter we discussed:

- the concept of inclusion and how it has evolved historically, legally and in practice;

- the legislative developments from 1978 to 2002, with a closer exploration of the revised *SEN Code of Practice* and the amended Disability Discrimination Act;

- the gradual move from 'integration' to 'inclusion', through examining the medical and social models of disability;

- general ways of ensuring exclusion does not occur in the early years setting, with relation to children with behavioural difficulties;

- some suggestions for developing inclusive practices.

Answers to 'Can you tell which is which?'

1   **Jason:** the medical model. Jenny's strategy of making him leave the play area until he learns to play properly reflects her perception that Jason is a 'naughty boy' and somehow deprivation of the toys will help him to learn appropriate play and social skills. She needs to plan a positive and practical step-by-step programme that will help Jason to develop these skills.

2   **Annan:** the social model. His practitioners have recognised that the sessions in the Large Hall cause problems and have taken steps to make sure Annan can join in and enjoy the activities for as long as he is able. The strategy of using the student to support him helps to reduce his stress and anxiety and therefore the inappropriate behaviour.

3   **Ned:** the medical model. The practitioners are totally focused on the age-related Foundation stage targets and if Ned fails to achieve some of them, he has to work below his age-related level until he does. It would be more appropriate to recognise and celebrate each of Ned's skills at his level of achievement and encourage him to develop them still further, even if this means working at different levels in the different areas of the curriculum.

4   **Minnie:** the medical model. Lily feels that the problem is within Minnie and is failing Minnie by depriving her of the opportunity to join in the discussions. Minnie is also deprived of the chance to learn speaking and listening skills. An uninterrupted session seems to be more of a priority than helping Minnie to develop.

5   **Hugh:** the social model. Hugh's practitioners recognise that the activity causes him problems and they devise a strategy that will enable him to join in the outings with support.

Answers to Quiz time

1 **Marco:** this is not inclusion. The setting needs to show both the parents and the other children that there is nothing to fear from Marco's difficulties. The practitioners need to encourage an ethos of welcoming all children, regardless of their difficulties, and to arrange the activities to enable Marco to take part without provoking bouts of inappropriate behaviour. There should be close liaison with Marco's parents and the relevant medical professionals to enable effective planning.

2 **Sophie:** this is inclusion. Sophie's practitioners have realised there's a pattern to her inappropriate behaviour – in the afternoons and probably because she's tired after a very early start. By adjusting Sophie's afternoon activities to take account of this (i.e. differentiating), the practitioners have ensured that she's included in the other things that are on offer.

3 **Pollyanna:** this is not inclusion. Pollyanna is being deprived of an activity that is on offer to the other children, and also of the chance to develop her speaking, listening, turn-taking and social skills. One practitioner could work with Pollyanna before the group session, explaining what it's going to be about and helping her to prepare her contribution. When Pollyanna becomes restless then the practitioner could withdraw her to the library, but encouraging her over a period of time to stay with the group for longer.

4 **Danny:** this is inclusion. The practitioners realise that Danny has difficulty in managing the beaker and is probably a bit overwhelmed by all the biscuits on one plate. By giving him a cup that he can use more easily and by changing the biscuit routine, Danny is included in snack time without the previous stresses.

PERSONA DOLLS

You can find a lot of useful information about using persona dolls, together with details about much of the relevant literature, by typing into your search engine 'Persona Dolls'. If you want to use the dolls specifically in regard to special educational needs and issues of disability and/or discrimination, Babette Brown works extensively in this field, to much acclaim, and offers training in the use of persona dolls. Contact details are as follows:

Telephone: 020 8446 7056
Fax: 020 8446 7591
e-mail: personadoll@ukgateway.net

References

1 & 2 Adapted from *All together, How to create inclusive services for disabled children and their families: a practical handbook for early years workers*, Mary Dickins and Judy Denziloe (London: National Children's Bureau 2003; 1st edn, London: National Early Years Network, 1998).

Chapter 2

How to write a positive behaviour policy for your setting

(or: Up Close and Positive)

In this chapter we will explore the rationale behind writing a positive behaviour policy by discussing:

- what a policy is, why it should be written and what should be in it;

- how adults involved with the setting should examine their own attitudes, beliefs and practices as part of the policy-planning process;

- how planning the policy should include everybody involved with the setting, especially the children and their parents;

- who puts the policy into practice and how.

All early years settings that receive government funding must write and put into practice a special educational needs (SEN) policy, but aside from the legal requirement, writing such a policy is an excellent way of reviewing practices and philosophy, and of focusing on inclusion. For this reason, private and non-maintained settings should also consider writing and implementing their own policies. Once the SEN policy is in place, you can use its framework to plan and write a positive behaviour policy. Some settings choose to subsume their positive behaviour policy into the SEN policy, but by planning and writing a separate policy for positive behaviour, practitioners can be more specific about how they want to approach the whole concept of positive behaviour, in ways that are appropriate for their setting and their children.

Before moving onto the positive behaviour policy in its own right, it's very useful to go back to basics and explore some fundamental aspects of policy making.

WHAT IS A POLICY?

Dickins and Denziloe (2003) say that a policy is a document that should:

- make a statement of the beliefs, values and goals of an organization;

- give a common message to workers, parents, children and anyone else who comes into contact with the service;

- broaden our horizons and help us to share good practice.[1]

In other words a policy is a **working document** produced by your setting to let everybody involved with the setting know what your aims are with regard to the children in your care. It is definitely not a document to quickly download from computer software, ready for next week's *Ofsted* inspection and then to be relegated to the back of a filing cabinet. Well-planned and carefully thought-through policies are a boon to practitioners, because they provide guidelines for good practice. A bit of hard work in the early stages of planning will mean much less hard work in the later stages of implementation.

WHY DOES YOUR SETTING NEED A POSITIVE BEHAVIOUR POLICY?

As inclusion becomes the norm, all early years settings have the care of some children with SEN in general, and some with behavioural difficulties in particular. Many practitioners have not specialised in this field and appreciate being able to refer to a positive behaviour policy as a basic guide for what is expected within their setting. There are many sound reasons why having a policy is good practice, among them are the following, which you may like to consider in relation to your own setting.

- As long as the policy is put into practice by everybody involved it helps to ensure the smooth running of the setting.

- By focusing on positive behaviour, the policy encourages caring attitudes by everybody towards each other and the environment.

- The policy helps to recognise and acknowledge everybody's place in and commitment to the setting.

- It also helps to ensure that everybody involved in the setting, including their opinions, is respected and valued.

- It offers support, help and encouragement to everybody in the setting, particularly if they feel unsure about how to work with a child who has behavioural difficulties.

- The policy helps to ensure a positive atmosphere where people (adults and children alike) who are involved in an incident can reflect on any injustice or injury and where possible make reparation.

WHAT NEEDS TO GO INTO A POSITIVE BEHAVIOUR POLICY?

The *SEN Code of Practice* suggests what you need to include in your SEN policy, but the same would apply to a positive behaviour policy. Among the most important are the following.

- *Information about the setting's provisions, including the aims and objectives of the policy.* In other words, you and your colleagues should ask yourselves, 'What are our aims in the code of conduct we are drawing up?' 'Are we aiming for inclusion of children with behavioural difficulties?' 'Does our policy make sure that happens?'

- *The name of the Special Educational Needs Coordinator (SENCO) and any specialities offered by members of staff.* So, if a practitioner within the setting has a qualification and/or training in the field of emotional and behavioural difficulties, they should be named in the policy, and what their speciality is. For example, 'Our SENCO, Clare Hardy, holds a B.Phil.Ed. and has specialised in working with children who have emotional and behavioural difficulties'.

- *The rules chosen by everybody in the setting.* These are the positive guidelines to be followed by everybody, children and adults alike, which were agreed at the planning stage of the policy. Including these in the policy also helps parents, carers and others who aren't in the setting all the time to ensure consistency by following the rules at home.

- *The methods agreed for encouraging positive behaviour.* This means the 'reward system' that has been agreed by everybody in the setting. There are many ways of doing this, from using stickers or star charts, to encouraging the children to monitor their own positive behaviour. There isn't a blueprint, since each setting and all children are unique, and the methods you all agree must be relevant to and appropriate for your setting and each child.

- *The agreed inappropriate behaviours.* The forms of unacceptable behaviour should be agreed by everybody in the setting and stated clearly in the policy. For example, any form of violence, physical excess such as snatching or pushing, bullying, name-calling, and so on.

- *The methods agreed on for sanctioning inappropriate behaviours.* In other words, the system that has been agreed by everybody in the setting, which is designed to discourage the agreed unacceptable behaviours.

- *The criteria for evaluating the success of the positive behaviour policy.* For this element of the policy, you should ask yourselves when and how the policy will be reviewed, how everybody will decide its strengths and weaknesses and how you will make any required changes. As the policy is used on a daily basis, its weaknesses will become apparent, how serious these are and how quickly they need to be addressed. Again, there is no blueprint because each setting is individual.

- *The arrangements for provision for children who have emotional and/or behavioural difficulties.* Questions to consider here include 'How are we going to support children with behavioural difficulties in terms of resources, staffing, time and so on?' You will have to look at the way the setting is organised, run, staffed and equipped, reviewing these and making sure each element includes children with behavioural difficulties, adapting them if necessary.

- *The arrangements for admission of children with behavioural difficulties.* For this you will need to agree your approach to how children with behavioural difficulties are admitted, whether you will have a transition or familiarisation period, whether you will invite parents to stay with the child initially, and so on.

- *The arrangements for identifying and assessing behavioural difficulties.* You will need to be clear about who will do the identification and assessments, when, where and how. It might be done by the child's own practitioner, the SENCO or the setting's head/manager. It could be done at a set time, or a time when the assessor happens to be 'free' to do it. You could decide it will be done either in the setting's usual daily activity sessions or during a special assessment/observation session. You need to agree what form the assessments will take and what will be used, for example, the Foundation stage profile, standardised assessments, observations (and what type of observation?) and so on.

- *The arrangements for providing support for children with behavioural difficulties.* This includes reviewing your resources and how you use them, whether the equipment, games and activities can be effectively and appropriately used by children with behavioural difficulties. For example, if Buster hates table-top activities and usually has a temper tantrum when he's asked to do them, while you're supporting him in controlling his feelings, give him other activities to do; if Buster's IEP says his reward is an extra session outside on the tricycles, make sure you have enough tricycles to go around; if Buster is usually tired in the afternoons when you have outside play, change the session to the morning when he's fresh and less likely to have a tantrum; if Buster has a problem working in big, open spaces, don't do drama in the main hall; if Buster would benefit from a cooking session, get Mrs Jennings, the volunteer who does cooking with some of the children, to squeeze in Buster as well.

- *The arrangements for providing access by the child with behavioural difficulties to a balanced and broadly based curriculum.* So you will need to ask yourselves how you will make sure that all the children, regardless of ability or the difficulties being experienced, have the opportunities and experiences of the full curriculum on offer, whether this is the Foundation stage or the National Curriculum. This may mean adjusting the timetable, the venue, the staffing, the resources and equipment and so on, to open up to the children with behavioural difficulties everything that's on offer to all the children. You should also review how you plan and implement Individual Education Plans, making sure that your procedures do actually result in effective support for each child.

- *The procedures for reviewing the needs of a child with behavioural difficulties.* So, when, where and how will reviews of each child's progress be carried out? Who will be involved? Some of the guidance in the *SEN Code of Practice* offers suggestions about these arrangements, but some things are unique to each setting. Because every setting has to consider its own facilities, timetable, staffing, clientele, and so on, in the decision-making, the agreed arrangements will be unique.

Some professionals advocate that a policy (any policy) should be no longer than one side of A4 paper. It's debatable whether those professionals have actually tried doing that, unless they used 8-point font and single spacing, written both horizontally and vertically on the page! However, if you feel that your policy is turning out to be a bit long for general consumption, you can shorten it, leaving out the fine details that are in the main policy, and offer a condensed version for those people who would prefer one. If the full version is requested and/or needed, you can issue or use it then, as appropriate. The full version would be made available to *Ofsted* inspectors or perhaps parents who are going to be involved in IEP planning for their child who has behavioural difficulties, while the condensed version may be made available to people who don't, at that point, want the full text. As long as you make sure everybody knows that the complete version is available whenever they want it, you will have met the needs of all concerned. Don't forget to consider whether you will need copies of the policy translated into other languages. If you do, make sure that the translation is of a high standard and accurate.

CAN YOU STAND UP TO SELF-SCRUTINY?

A fundamental part of planning and writing a positive behaviour policy is for us as practitioners to think honestly and deeply about our own attitudes towards, beliefs about and ways of working with children who have behavioural difficulties. This might make us uncomfortable, if we're truthful with ourselves, because we can all think of times when we've been less than understanding of a child who was behaving inappropriately, and who was managing to irritate us. The child we decided was 'just a spiteful little devil' was probably short-changed by us, maybe by having less of our attention, input or understanding. The child we negatively categorised because they came from a different area or background from ourselves may well have been unfairly judged as 'typical of somebody from that estate'. The child who constantly challenged our patience probably ended up being sidelined while we worked with a child whom we considered was more deserving of our time and attention.

We have to be professional enough to step back from the emotional reactions we may have and try to understand why the child is behaving as they are, then do something about it. Occasionally, it's *our* reactions and interactions with a child that can be the cause of some of their behavioural difficulties. When this happens, we must have sufficient integrity to acknowledge it, and change our approach to the child.

━━━━▶ **ACTIVITY**

Answer these questions as honestly as you can.

1 As a child, what did you think was 'bad' behaviour?

2 What happened to children who behaved badly?

3 How did you feel when you saw other children behaving badly?

4 Did you ever behave badly yourself?

5 What happened as a result? How were you punished?

6 How did you feel at the time about the way you were punished for behaving badly?

7 As an adult, what do you consider to be inappropriate behaviour for (a) children and (b) adults?

8 Do you ever still behave in a way you might consider to be inappropriate?

9 Think about a particular child you have worked with, who has irritated you – what were your negative feelings about their behaviour?

10 How did the child particularly irritate you – what did they do that annoyed you?

11 Did that child remind you of anybody you knew? How?

12. Think of something that was *likeable* about the child as a person: what they liked to do, what made them laugh, what they were good at, and so on.

13 Make a list of the ways you refer to children in your setting who have behaved inappropriately. What names or labels have you used? Did you ever use them to the child directly? (For example, 'You're a very naughty boy, Buster!') Which names did you use jokingly or affectionately? Which did you use when you were annoyed with the child and were, in essence, insulting them (whether privately to yourself or another member of staff)? How would you feel if you discovered that somebody you know had referred to you using those names? [2]

CASE STUDY

Mrs Jones found it very difficult to tolerate Robert's behaviour as she felt he was a disruptive influence in her room. She was working with 25 4- to 5-year olds, with a Learning Support Assistant, Maria. She often told Maria in front of the other children she thought it wasn't fair that Robert took so much of their time from the others and also that Robert was just a naughty boy.

Some of the other children discovered that spoiling Robert's game on the computer usually caused him to lose his temper and one day Benjamin did it deliberately to provoke Robert. Maria saw what happened and also that this time Robert didn't

CONTINUED

retaliate but went to Mrs Jones to complain. Without listening to what Robert had to say, Mrs Jones immediately began to tell Robert off, ending with 'You're just a nasty piece of work and always will be'. Robert's reaction was to throw himself on the floor, scream and kick his legs. Mrs Jones looked at Maria and said, 'Well – what else do you expect?'

Here we see a practitioner failing a child in her care. Rather than trying to find out what may be at the root of Robert's difficulties, she labels him as 'just a naughty boy'. She publicly criticises him and on an occasion when she should be supporting him, she not only doesn't do this but she actually launches into another reprimand that's unjustified. Mrs Jones may be feeling unsupported, stressed and exasperated, so she needs to take time out to review her situation. She and Robert may be causing each other's difficulties in the way they interact, so trying to find a new way of working together may ease the situation. Maria could help here by doing some activities with Robert when Mrs Jones feels she needs some time away from him. By limiting her discussions of Robert to a time and a place when both he and the other children aren't present, Mrs Jones will have less chance to exaggerate the problem. Maria can direct their discussions to a more positive level by helping Mrs Jones to look objectively at what Robert's difficulties are, what seems to trigger them, and what strategies they can put in place to support Robert. The child's parents can be approached to become involved in a plan of action to help Robert to overcome his difficulties. If Mrs Jones needs support herself, she should approach the setting's manager for an opportunity to attend professional development training in the area of behavioural difficulties.

Sometimes, it may be the way we interact with other adults within the setting that affects a child. We can easily forget how deeply we influence the young children in our care, by what we say and, crucially, by what we do. They're watching our behaviour and if we're not excellent role models, then we have only our own inappropriate behaviour to blame when the children imitate us. While we are usually extremely careful to behave appropriately towards the children, and keen to show the children how to behave appropriately towards each other, we can sometimes overlook the way we behave towards other adults. Young children are very quick to pick up on atmosphere and to copy what adults do, and if we treat another adult less courteously than we should, we are acting as poor role models. During your self-examination session, ask yourself the following questions.

1   Do I get along with every adult involved with the setting (including the parents)? If not, who is it I find difficult to interact with?

2   What is it I dislike about that person? Why do I dislike them?

3   Could there be something about me that they dislike?

4   Do I make a real effort to treat that person with respect? Do I sometimes ignore them, refuse to speak to them or turn away from them?

5   Do I sometimes speak sharply to that person? If so, is it in front of anybody else, particularly the children?

6   Do I discuss that person with other adults in the setting? Do I do this in front of the children?

7   Is there some way that person may need support and I'm failing to give it?

8   Do I really make an effort not to show my negative feelings to that person? Do I go out of my way to behave positively towards them?

Obviously, in any work situation, there are times when problems with other people arise and there are incidents, practices or situations that have to be addressed and sorted out. Personnel issues or crises such as these should be dealt with as they arise by the people involved, possibly with the setting's manager(s) and, hopefully, don't occur on a regular basis. But the daily interaction between the adults in the setting and the way their relationships are conducted is part of the running of the setting, and it is crucial that these are harmonious.

If you feel that your relationship with the other adults in the setting is positive, the next thing to look at is whether you and they behave in the same way as you expect the children to behave. For example, if the children are discouraged from shouting inside, avoid falling into the trap of calling across the room, 'Mary, while you're in the store cupboard, will you bring me some more blue paint, please?' because it's convenient just at that moment; or if the children aren't allowed to throw things indoors, make the effort to go to the opposite side of the table to give the rubber to Buster, rather than toss it across to him.

It's the simple avoidance of 'Do as I say, not as I do' – make sure the children have positive behaviour to imitate because they'll just as quickly imitate the negative aspects.

CASE STUDY

Mrs Barrington had been appointed Nursery Deputy Manager in preference to Mrs Smith who had applied for the job from within the setting's staff. Mrs Smith was bitterly disappointed that she didn't get the job and took an instant dislike to Mrs Barrington. She was overheard telling another practitioner in the setting that she had no intention of 'kowtowing to that woman', even before Mrs Barrington took up her post.

As Mrs Barrington began to make changes and introduce innovations in the setting, with the support of the Manager, Mrs Smith became uncooperative. Her attitude towards Mrs Barrington became disrespectful in staff meetings and hostile in their one-to-one interactions. She began to make complaints to the Manager about Mrs Barrington, and encouraged other staff members to make life difficult for the new Deputy Manager. Eventually, the situation became so uncomfortable that the staff became divided into two factions, those supporting Mrs Smith and those backing Mrs Barrington. This created a tense and unhappy atmosphere in the setting that the children picked up on – one child was heard to tell another that 'Mrs Smith hates Mrs Barrington and my Mum says she doesn't know why'. Clearly the parents now knew what was going on in the setting.

Here we have a situation that should never have been allowed to get so out of hand. When Mrs Smith failed to get the job, the Manager of the setting should have immediately supported her either by offering her alternative responsibilities within the setting, or the opportunity for further professional training and development that would have helped future career moves. Mrs Smith may have felt threatened by Mrs Barrington and the only way she knew of coping with this was to try to undermine her with other members of staff. Mrs Barrington should have tried to involve Mrs Smith in the planning and development of some of the innovations she was putting in place. The other members of staff should have avoided becoming involved in the differences between the two women. The saddest part of the tale is that the feud trickled out to the children and their parents. How can they have confidence in what the practitioners are doing if they see the staff behaving no better than children themselves? It seems that a more mature attitude by everybody was needed in this setting.

WHO PLANS AND USES THE POLICY?

Everybody appropriately involved with the setting should be included in the planning and use of the policy. This also means the children. The *SEN Code of Practice* emphasises the involvement of the children where possible in planning and putting into practice anything that affects their progress. This should also apply to planning positive behaviour policies.

Ownership of the final document is the result of involvement in the planning, and this ownership means that everybody has a vested interest in its success. The inclusion of everybody in the setting in the planning, design implementation, and review of the policy is more likely to achieve success.

'Everybody' means the children, the parents or carers, the practitioners, outside agents who are involved with the setting, governors or managers if appropriate, and other adults within the setting such as lunchtime supervisors, club or activity organisers, taxi-escorts and so on. Each person's opinion and ideas need to be listened to and, if agreed, included in the final draft.

HOW DO WE GO ABOUT IT?

Think of a ripple effect. Start from the core of the setting – you and the children – and work outwards, taking in the feedback from all the other parties. You may choose to do this by holding a series of formal meetings, by issuing question-naires, by informal chats, and so on. You will know what approach is the best for your setting. There are some basic elements that need to go into the first draft(s) of your policy.

- Discuss and choose some positive 'house rules' for the children to follow and others for the practitioners to implement. Do this together with the children and the adults who work with them.

- Let the children help to decide on their rules. Keep them positive, just a few and fairly simple. For example:

  1 We are kind to each other.
  2 We walk when we are inside.
  3 We tidy up when we have finished.

  These are more positive than the following version of the same rules:

  1 Don't be unkind to each other.
  2 Don't run around when you are inside.
  3 Don't leave your things lying around.

  'Don't' is a negative form of language and can give the impression that every thing in the setting 'isn't allowed'.

- Keep the adults' rules positive and simple too, because the children will also need to know them. For example:

  1 When the children are playing outside an adult must be there.
  2 Adults may shout for children only when they are outside.
  3 Adults must make sure that no more than four children are in the water play at the same time.

- Decide on the methods to use for modifying unacceptable behaviour. Again, everybody should be involved in making these decisions. It's useful to have several approaches and one at least should work for each child. Some examples might be

  i Ignore the unacceptable behaviour.

  ii Remove the child from the situation where the behaviour is occurring.

  iii Distract the child with a different activity, game or toy.

  iv Avoid 'telling off' the child for every little misdemeanour – let some things go.

v Acknowledge and praise every example of the child's positive behaviour, no matter how brief. Be specific when you do this: 'Buster, I saw you helping Ellie put on her coat; you're a very kind boy'.

vi Keep the child out of situations you know create problems. For example, if Buster can't sit still for more than three minutes, choose shorter books for story session.

● Decide when to review the policy. If you are putting the policy into place for the first time, you should give it about a term or so (three to four months) to see whether it's working appropriately and effectively in your setting. If the policy has already had at least one review, keep monitoring any weaknesses that were identified at the original review and how these were to be addressed. If there still seem to be problems, review the policy again quickly, to decide ways of eliminating the difficulties.

INVOLVING THE CHILDREN IN THE PLANNING PROCESS

'Children who are capable of forming views, have a right to receive and make known information, to express an opinion, and to have that opinion taken into account in any matters affecting them. The views of the child should be given due weight according to the age, maturity and capability of the child.'

(Articles 12 and 13, *United Nations Convention on the Rights of the Child*, 1989)

Children, even young ones, have relevant and important information about themselves and their view of their situation, and this is what lies behind the UN statement above.

As practitioners, we have a responsibility to listen to this information and to wisely and lovingly use it to enable the children to fulfil their potential. We can do this through careful, cooperative planning, 'cooperative' being the key word. For example, you can say to the children, 'We're all going to decide on a plan that makes sure everyone in our nursery behaves kindly to each other. Can you think of some good ideas to include in our plan?'

You can then thought-shower with the children and pick up on whichever of their suggestions are useful and relevant – it can be surprising what they come up with!

It is important that during these discussions you make sure none of the children focuses on a particular child who has a behaviour difficulty, because the policy has to be a *general document*. You can deflect the direction of the conversation by saying something like, 'At the moment Buster's working hard on being kind to everybody. Now what about Jason's idea of taking turns to tidy up – is that a good rule to choose?'

Sometimes you may be working with a child whose problems are so profound and complex that they will find it very difficult to take part in the process of planning and decision-making, but where they can be involved it's important that you make sure this happens.

The children need to

- *Understand the importance of information.* To make any decision, whether it is a choice between playing in the water or reading a book, or what should be included in the positive behaviour policy, information is needed. The child's choice between playing in the water or reading a book may be influenced by the fact that they love books or hate water-play, (or indeed the opposite), the type of books on offer, the toys that are in the water tray, or even the temperature of the water.

  The 'consumers' who will be using the positive behaviour policy, and this includes the children, should have an influence on what goes into it. As practitioners therefore, we must show the children that information is a vital element in the planning of the policy. Sharing with them why we need the policy and the type of things that should be in it are important ways of involving them in its creation.

- *Express their feelings.* The Foundation stage curriculum includes this and rightly so. If the children are to grow into adults who can communicate effectively and confidently, they must be encouraged at this stage of their development to say what they feel. You should try to create an atmosphere where the children feel comfortable enough to say what they feel about something, even when what they're saying is not what you would have expected. How they're feeling should be respected. It's crucial that this becomes an automatic part of any speaking and listening session, whether planned or spontaneous.

- *Participate in discussions.* This follows on from the previous point. If the children have confidence in expressing their feelings, they will also naturally take an active part in discussions without being uncomfortable. Their contribution to discussions should be valued and respected, even if their opinion goes against that of the majority of the other children. What a child has suggested may not be included in the final draft or decision, but as the adults, we need to show that what the child offered has been a valuable element in reaching the agreed decision; in other words, part of the information-gathering process.

- *Indicate their choices.* Few children have a problem with indicating their choices! They should feel relaxed enough to say what they want and, where possible, you should encourage them to say why they want it. They won't be able to develop all these skills by themselves; we need to help them along the way.

The adults need to

- *Give the children information and support.* As we have already discussed, the children need information to take part in the decision-making process. It is our responsibility to make sure they get it.

   We regularly hear the phrases 'informed choices' and 'informed decisions' in relation to our right to information for our decision-making. Children have as much right to information concerning something that fundamentally affects them.

   Similarly, they have a right to our support in their learning how to make their decisions, even those we may not agree with ourselves.

- *Provide an appropriate and supportive environment.* It isn't enough for one or two practitioners to offer support – everybody in the setting must do so. In this way, a supportive ethos will be created within the setting that will enable the children to develop the self-confidence they need to express their feelings, opinions and needs.

   Children learn through example. As practitioners, we must model respect for others by listening to children's contributions, by acknowledging them and valuing them, in front of the other children.

- *Learn how to listen to the children.* The importance of helping a child to develop their speaking and listening skills is well documented and cannot be emphasised enough. Unfortunately, as practitioners we often need a good lesson in listening. With the best of intentions, and without realising it, we often talk far too much both at the children and to them, often not giving them a proper chance to talk to and with us. It can be a sobering experience to monitor ourselves and realise just how many of our conversations with the children consist of question and answer sessions, and how many of those questions require just one word answers.

INVOLVING THE PARENTS OR CARERS IN THE PLANNING PROCESS

'Partnership with parents plays a key role in promoting a culture of co-operation between parents, schools, LEAs and others. This is important in enabling children and young people with SEN to achieve their potential.'

(DfES, 2001:16) [3]

Often as practitioners, we fail to be sensitive to the feelings of parents of children who have behavioural difficulties. If you can think of a child in your setting who causes you a headache with their inappropriate behaviour, imagine what the child's family may be going through. It is vital to understand, support and involve them. This includes consulting them and asking for their input when planning the positive behaviour policy. They often have valuable suggestions and contributions to make to the general discussion, and can suggest good practical ideas that are worth putting into practice.

But this doesn't mean that you approach only the parents of children with behavioural difficulties for their input to the policy. The parents of all the children have the right to be consulted and included, and again, they can offer valuable insight and ideas that you may not have thought of.

Effective parental involvement

This happens in settings where practitioners do the following.

- *Encourage parental influence on the development of the setting's management, policies and practice.* The success of the positive behaviour policy depends on this parental involvement. The children do not live in compartments where what happens in the setting is separate from what happens at home. The two environments are inextricably linked and the child moves between them seamlessly. Without the support of the parents, the policy is less likely to work; with their input, it's more likely to work. You may need to ask parents of a child with behavioural difficulties to put the policy into practice at home, so giving the child consistency. If the policy is imposed on them and is something they haven't had any prior involvement with, they will be less inclined to cooperate with you, and understandably so.

- *Develop parent-friendly policies.* This speaks for itself. Sometimes there are barriers in the parents' minds and parent-friendly policies can go a long way to breaking these down. Such barriers can exist for quite a few reasons. For example, they may see you as 'authority' (in a negative sense), even as a source of the power to have 'my kids taken away from me'; they may have had bad experiences at school as youngsters and therefore don't have any trust in teachers or education practitioners of any kind; they may have had poor quality service up to now from other 'professionals' and think that you're a bird of the same feather. It is vital that you show the parents that everybody is working towards the same target: the welfare and development of the children. By getting them on board during the early stages of policy planning you will go a long way towards this.

- *Respect the parents' views.* The child will have made great strides in their development before they came to your setting, and their parents will have played a fundamental role in this. As practitioners, we must acknowledge the parents as the experts in their child and listen to their views and opinions. They can often give us an important clue into how we can make sure the child's needs are met. In the same way that respecting the children's views and opinions is important, acknowledging the value of their parents' views and opinions is a fundamental part of a positive and cooperative relationship.

INVOLVING OUTSIDE AGENTS IN THE PLANNING PROCESS

The setting doesn't become a sealed unit every morning once the children are all inside. There are people coming in and out for a variety of reasons, from the taxi escort to the educational psychologist to the local religious practitioner. Each of these people has something to offer from their particular viewpoint, and should be asked for their opinion.

So who exactly are these outside agents and which ones would be relevant to a positive behaviour policy? They come from a range of services including the following.

- *Education.* This would include the Local Education Authority's (LEA's) support service for children with emotional and behavioural difficulties and the educational psychological service.

- *Health.* Here you could include health visitors, paediatric nurses and/or paediatricians, nurses, community or hospital-based paediatricians, child psychiatrists, GPs, and hospital-based counsellors.

- *Social services and child protection services.* Social workers, education welfare officers, police child protection officers and possibly attached child psychologists may be included in this group

- *Private or voluntary organisations including self-help and support groups.*

- *Governors,* if appropriate for your setting.

You may be asking why you would involve outside agents in planning a policy for your setting – is it any of their business? As early years practitioners, we have the experience and expertise gained from an overview of the wider early years picture. The usual reason for consulting outside agents is because we don't have the expertise needed to work with particular difficulties, in this case, behavioural difficulties. If we're less confident in our knowledge of a specialised field, or even if we have an SEN qualification in a different field of difficulty, the policy is likely to reflect this. By asking for the input of those outside agents who are specialists in other areas your policy will have a specialised element that makes it more likely to be successful.

You might then ask what their involvement would be. That really depends on you, your setting and what you want your policy to include.

The *LEA support services* can provide advice on management and teaching techniques and strategies, setting management, curriculum materials, curriculum development, direct teaching or practical support for practitioners, part-time specialist help, or access to learning support assistance. You should have contact details for these services. If you don't, the SEN section of the LEA will be able to supply the relevant details, circulars and information.

The *educational psychology service* can carry out more specialised assessments, suggest problem solving strategies, including techniques in managing behaviour, and evaluating individual children's progress. They can also offer information and advice about the development of the positive behaviour policy and help you with the professional development of staff in this area of special educational needs, as well as helping with promoting inclusion.

The *health services* can offer advice and support in the management of conditions that may be connected to behavioural difficulties such as Attention Deficit Disorder. Make sure you tap this advice and support without focusing on a particular child – that should be part of their Individual Education Plan.

Social services and/or child protection services will work closely with you to support the child who may be experiencing problems from within the family. This can range, for example, from them working with parents on positive parenting skills, to the police child protection officers dealing with abuse of the child whether that's physical, emotional or sexual, or even a combination. Any or all of these problems can contribute to the child's behavioural difficulties.

Private or voluntary organizations do wonderful work in their fields and because of their specialised knowledge they are a valuable source of help and information. It is helpful to them if you download information from their websites to keep their postal costs down. You can almost always access the address or contact details by using your search engine.

Governors of early years settings are usually heavily and actively involved in the standards and quality of the setting. They play another important part in the workings of an early years setting, and if your setting has governors, you should involve them in your policy planning. By making sure they have both the knowledge and understanding of what is going on in your setting, you will be enabling them to make a valuable and relevant contribution to the policy, offering advice from their perspective.

A sentence or two outlining the type of support and liaison that your setting has with each of the involved outside agents will be sufficient for the policy document.

HOW TO PUT YOUR PLANNING INTO PRACTICE

- *Ensure that the children and all the adults in the setting can communicate effectively.* This really can't be emphasised enough. Many differences, misunderstandings and problems can be sorted out in the early stages with effective communication. It is very important that everybody living together in the setting communicates with each other, so you need to make sure that everybody's speaking and listening skills are put to good use, the adults' as well as children's.

- *Ensure that the children respect and value each other's opinions.* We have already touched on how adults must value the children's viewpoints but it is also crucial to highlight the importance of making sure that the children's opinions are respected and valued *by the other children* as well.

   It is vital to show this by the example of the adults within the setting, and to discourage any attempts by the children to belittle what other children might have to say. Be aware too that you may have to watch out for other adults in the setting who are less sensitive to this side of things.

- *Ensure that everybody implements and reviews the policy.* The day-to-day operation of the policy is everybody's responsibility and is a fundamental part of making the policy work. Everybody putting the policy into practice means it is more likely to work. It will also ensure that those children who are experiencing behavioural difficulties will have the consistency and stability that is so vital for them. Constant reviewing will ensure its strengths are kept and its weaknesses removed.

We can see, then, that the **planning, writing, publishing and reviewing** of the policy should include everybody appropriately involved with the setting; the **management** of the policy is the manager or head's responsibility; the day-to-day **operation** of the policy is the Special Educational Needs Coordinator's (SENCO) responsibility and the actual **implementation** of the policy is the responsibility of all other involved adults within their own area.

It's all about total ownership and everybody should ensure the policy is being implemented. It's through the day-to-day practicalities of using the policy that its strengths and weaknesses will be shown up. So the 'hands-on' people have a crucial role to play by continually thinking about how the policy works well and where it has weaknesses, and, most importantly, by telling the SENCO or the appropriate person what they have discovered.

Liz Wilcock (2001) cleverly sums up policy planning in a nutshell, as follows:

Ask yourselves the following questions:

- Why do we need it?

- Who is it for?

- What needs to be in it?

- How should it be worded?

- When will it be used?

- Where do we start? [4]

and continually bear in mind that the policy should be

- Relevant

- Owned

- Practised

- Reviewed. [5]

You will find an example of a short positive behaviour policy on page 38 and a full-length version on pages 39–40. You can adapt either of them for your own setting as you think appropriate.

QUIZ TIME

| Figure 2.1 | Tick the appropriate boxes. You may like to tick more than one box. |

When a setting creates its positive behaviour policy, who	Children	Manager/ Head	SENCO	Practitioner	Outside agent(s)	Parents/ carers	Other(s) If so, who?
plans it?							
writes it?							
publishes it?							
manages it?							
operates it?							
implements it?							
reviews it?							

For answers see Figure 2.2 on page 37.

SUMMARY

In this chapter we discussed:

- what a positive behaviour policy is, why it should be written and what should be in it, especially all the salient points;

- that planning the policy should include everybody involved with the setting, especially the children and their parents;

- that practitioners within the setting should examine their own attitudes, beliefs and practices during the policy-planning process;

- who implements the policy and how, ensuring it is positive, user-friendly and workable, highlighting the behaviours to be encouraged and the inappropriate behaviours to be discouraged, and agreeing on rewards and sanctions.

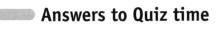 Answers to Quiz time

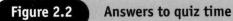

Figure 2.2　Answers to quiz time

When a setting creates its positive behaviour policy, who	Children	Manager/ Head	SENCO	Practitioner	Outside agent(s)	Parents/ carers	Other(s) If so, who?
plans it?	✔	✔	✔	✔	✔	✔	✔
writes it?	✔	✔	✔	✔	✔	✔	✔
publishes it?	✔	✔	✔	✔	✔	✔	✔
manages it?		✔					
operates it?			✔				
implements it?		*	*	✔			*
reviews it?	✔	✔	✔	✔	✔	✔	✔

* If the Manager/Head, SENCO and/or other adults are also 'frontline practitioners' who are actually putting the policy into practice, these boxes would need a tick as well.

AN EXAMPLE OF AN EARLY YEARS POSITIVE BEHAVIOUR POLICY (SHORT VERSION)

High Fells Nursery Positive Behaviour Policy

We believe that all children, including those with behavioural difficulties, have the right to a broad, balanced and purposeful early years curriculum. Our intention is to ensure the inclusion of all the children in our nursery.

Our SENCO is Clare Hardy and she helps everybody involved with our nursery in all aspects of supporting children with behavioural difficulties and their families.

Clare has completed the LEA's accredited course in supporting children with emotional and behavioural difficulties.

Our aim is to

- ensure a happy, caring and secure environment for everybody who works in or visits High Fells Nursery;
- ensure that everybody in our setting, their opinions and their talents are respected and valued;
- identify children's behavioural difficulties, and to work together with their parents to support the children in managing their difficulties;
- differentiate, adapt and accommodate our curriculum, activities and materials when necessary, to ensure the inclusion of children with behavioural difficulties;
- ensure that our plans for each child with behavioural difficulties are appropriate;
- review at least once a month, with parents, their child's action plan(s) and make appropriate changes when necessary;
- emphasise and encourage positive behaviour by everybody in the setting;
- identify behaviours that are acceptable and agree on ways to encourage these within the setting;
- identify behaviours that are unacceptable and decide on ways of discouraging and/or managing these within the setting;
- acknowledge when we cannot meet the child's needs in High Fells Nursery and to discuss with their parents the request of support from outside professionals;
- work together with the outside professionals, the child and the parents to plan and use appropriately revised individual educational programmes (IEPs) to support the child;
- acknowledge when we continue to be unable to meet the child's needs in High Fells Nursery, and to discuss, with everybody involved, a request to the LEA for a statutory assessment of the child;
- review this policy once each term and make any appropriate changes to ensure it is relevant to our setting and the children we care for.

AN EXAMPLE OF AN EARLY YEARS POSITIVE BEHAVIOUR POLICY (FULL-LENGTH VERSION)

High Fells Nursery Positive Behaviour Policy

We believe that all children, including those with behavioural difficulties, have the right to a broad, balanced and purposeful early years curriculum. Our intention is to ensure the inclusion of all the children in our nursery.

Our SENCO is Clare Hardy and she

- helps us to identify children's behavioural difficulties;
- helps us with planning approaches to working with and supporting children with behavioural difficulties;
- updates the parents with their children's progress;
- makes sure the children's progress is regularly reviewed;
- makes sure the parents are fully involved with the planning for their child.

Clare has completed the LEA's accredited course in supporting children with emotional and behavioural difficulties.

Our aim is to

- ensure a happy, caring and secure environment for everybody who works in or visits High Fells Nursery;
- ensure that everybody in our setting, their opinions and their talents are respected and valued;
- admit children with behavioural difficulties after a familiarisation period which is appropriate to the child's needs; parents may stay with the child initially, according to the needs of the child;
- identify children's behavioural difficulties using a variety of observations, assessments and monitoring procedures, according to the child's needs; assessments and identification of behavioural difficulties will be done by the appropriate member(s) of staff; parents will be involved with and informed of each assessment;
- work together with parents to support the children in managing their difficulties, deciding on programmes or plans of action according to each child's needs;
- differentiate, adapt and accommodate our curriculum, activities and materials when necessary, to ensure the inclusion of children with behavioural difficulties; any adaptations will be made according to the needs of the child;
- ensure that our plans for each child with behavioural difficulties are appropriate, closely monitoring their progress to make sure that the plans remain appropriate and relevant;

- review at least once a month, with parents, their child's action plan(s) and make appropriate changes when necessary;

- emphasise and encourage positive behaviour by everybody in the setting; this includes adults as well as children;

- identify behaviours that are acceptable and agree on ways to encourage these within the setting, for example by drawing attention to and publicly praising children when they show positive behaviour; these ways should be appropriate and meaningful for each child;

- identify behaviour that is unacceptable, for example, swearing, bullying or physical violence;

- decide on ways of discouraging and/or managing these unacceptable behaviours within the setting, for example by ignoring the undesired behaviour or by withholding 'free choice' activities; these ways should be appropriate and meaningful for each child;

- acknowledge when we cannot meet the child's needs in High Fells Nursery and to discuss with their parents the request for support from outside professionals;

- work together with the outside professionals, the child and the parents to plan and use appropriately revised individual educational plans (IEPs) to support the child;

- regularly review the IEPs to ensure that they remain appropriate and effective for the child's progress;

- acknowledge when we continue to be unable to meet the child's needs in High Fells Nursery, and to discuss, with everybody involved, a request to the LEA for a statutory assessment of the child;

- review this policy once each term and make any appropriate changes to ensure it is relevant to our setting and the children we care for.

References

1 *All Together, How to create inclusive services for disabled children and their families, a practical handbook for early years workers*, M. Dickins and J. Denziloe (National Children's Bureau 2003; 1st edn, National Early Years Network, 1998).

2 Adapted from *Inclusion in Early Years Disability Equality in Education Course Book*, (Disability Equality in Education, 2002).

3 Special Educational Needs Code of Practice. (DfES, 2001).

4 and 5 'Policies and procedures', Liz Wilcock (*Practical Pre-school*, July 2001).

Chapter 3

How to write Individual Education Plans to encourage positive behaviour

(or: 'A Personal Matter')

This chapter will explore the concept of differentiating the curriculum for the child with behavioural difficulties who needs to follow a programme that is *additional* to and *different from* the usual early years curriculum, in line with the *SEN Code of Practice*. We will

- look at ways of identifying and recording inappropriate behaviour, particularly through observations;

- examine some general principles behind the planning and writing of Individual Education Plans (IEPs);

- explore the writing of IEPs specifically for children with behavioural difficulties;

- look at ways of working with the child and their parents in the planning and implementation of an IEP;

- discuss the holistic approach to planning IEPs;

- look at the practicalities involved in reviewing IEPs.

There is no blueprint or standard format for writing IEPs because every child is unique. Even two or more children with similar difficulties, or even the same condition (for example, AD/HD or autism), will learn, develop and progress differently and so will not be able to share a common IEP. There are software programmes available that 'write' IEPs and it's very tempting to believe you can save time and effort by using these to print out an instant IEP. The reality is that you will be wasting precious money in buying the software because you'll discover in time that the IEP is simply not supporting the child or helping them to develop. By then, the child has lost precious time and you'll probably still be wondering what on earth you can do to help them. Another, more important, reason for avoiding computer-generated IEPs is that, by using them, the practitioner will not have planned the programme together with the child, the child's parents and anybody else who is involved. As we shall see in this chapter, the close involvement and cooperation of everybody concerned throughout the planning and implementation of the IEP is vital.

In the early stages after identifying a difficulty, you must take the time to plan an IEP with the child's specific needs in mind: in other words, a tailor-made programme, possible only through knowing the child well and talking to others about them and what makes them tick.

CASE STUDY

A nursery in a northern city had a high number of children experiencing behavioural difficulties. The nursery was in a deprived area of the city and many of the children came from troubled or difficult families, with drug abuse and crime a normal part of their daily lives.

The practitioner grouped together four children who, in her opinion, were experiencing the same type of behaviour difficulty, because they were all inclined to throw tantrums and become aggressive towards other children. This group of children stayed together for most of the day to do their activities and they were all following the same (computer-generated) IEP, with identical targets to work towards.

A student nursery nurse on placement in the setting was concerned about the situation. She asked the practitioner whether the IEP was effective for all the children, and was told that it seemed to be, although there were still problems with the children. The practitioner also commented that it was much easier for her to print out one IEP and write the names of the four children at the top, than to print out four copies of the same IEP and 'waste time' (her words) filling one in for each child.

The student told her tutor at college, who confirmed that IEPs should indeed be written for each child, hence the name *Individual* Education Plan. Unfortunately, the situation was difficult because the nursery offered a valuable placement opportunity for the students which the college was reluctant to jeopardise, and also because the tutor, as an 'outsider', felt she had no right to question the practices of another professional in a setting that wasn't her own.

In the end, the tutor spoke to the nursery's Head, who was also the SENCO, and who wasn't aware of the joint IEP. As the nursery was just beginning to plan its SEN policy, the Head made arrangements for all the practitioners to attend special needs training, and gave close support to the practitioner who was using the joint IEP. When the next batch of students was on placement in the setting, the tutor found that the practitioner was indeed using Individual Education Plans, and was planning them appropriately, consulting with everybody involved.

If a child enters your setting and immediately starts to behave in ways that you find unacceptable, it's important that you don't immediately jump to the conclusion that you have a child here with behavioural difficulties.

The child may come from a home environment that sees pushing and wrestling with other children as a form of play. You will need to show the child how to play appropriately and what sort of behaviour you expect of them within the setting.

The child may be at a stage of development where they still find it hard to control their impulses and simply can't help themselves when it comes to physical exuberance. They might still need to touch things and explore with their hands, which you may prefer them not to do sometimes.

Their language and communication skills may still be developing and they may have no idea what you mean when you use terms or words that are intended to encourage them to behave in an acceptable way. They may have difficulties in keeping still or in concentrating for longer than a minute or two, and they may find it hard to look and listen.

For some children, coming to an early years setting is the first time they've been away from home and their loved ones. The separation alone may be so hard for them to handle that they react in the only way they know. They may even find it hard to meet with new children and new adults.

All of these factors can mean stress for the child, and so we need to make allowances in the early days after admission. Give the child time to settle in, to get to know your routine, to learn the parameters and what exactly you want and expect of them. One of your best resources in this situation is the child's parents. Talk to them and ask them for any hints or suggestions for helping the child to settle in. Don't be too hasty in deciding that the child has behavioural difficulties until you've given them a fair chance.

Some children have a low self-esteem and this definitely influences the way they behave. Poor self-esteem goes hand in hand with a lack of confidence, and the behaviour of such a child follows a clear pattern. Hannah Mortimer (2000) shows this very well as follows:

Children who have low self-esteem often:

- have a strong need for reassurance
- appear to feel insecure
- seem to feel safer if they 'take control'
- seem to have no faith in their own capabilities
- have problems learning
- are reluctant to express their opinions

CONTINUED

- find it hard to accept correction
- find it hard to make decisions
- tend to overreact to failure
- have a low opinion of themselves
- tend to hurt or bully others[1]

It becomes clear then that we need to help the child to develop a high self-esteem in order to counteract these negative outcomes. By providing an environment that is positive, supportive, warm and welcoming, and that values the child for themselves, we can make inroads on raising their self-esteem and try to reduce the child's inappropriate behaviours.

The other side of the coin shows a child with equally clear and observable behaviours as a result of high self-esteem. Here's Hannah Mortimer again:

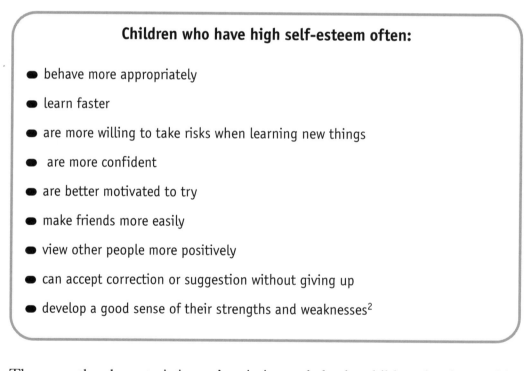

Children who have high self-esteem often:

- behave more appropriately
- learn faster
- are more willing to take risks when learning new things
- are more confident
- are better motivated to try
- make friends more easily
- view other people more positively
- can accept correction or suggestion without giving up
- develop a good sense of their strengths and weaknesses[2]

These are the characteristics we're aiming to help the child to develop and by focusing on their needs and planning an appropriate and relevant IEP, we should be going some way to meeting our aims.

It may be that when you've allowed a realistic length of time for the child to settle with you, and have differentiated your approaches to help them develop positive behaviours, you still have concerns about them. This will be the stage at which you decide to discuss the situation with everybody and plan an IEP.

So where do you start? The first thing you need to do is be specific about what you mean by the child's 'inappropriate behaviour', and an effective way of doing this is through observations.

IDENTIFYING AND RECORDING INAPPROPRIATE BEHAVIOUR

In order to plan an effective IEP that targets and meets the child's needs, you need information about the child. You have to find out what are their areas of need, but you also need to identify their strengths, because those strengths are going to be your starting point. The best technique to use for gathering information about young children is observation. Fortunately this is recognised by the DfES which has highlighted its value and importance in assessing and monitoring early years children. There's a variety of ways you can make your observations, but whichever method you choose, it is important that the information you gather is accurate. Some settings use standardised checklists which have been validated through trials and formalised use, and the information gleaned through these certainly is useful. To focus on particular areas of a child's behaviour, many practitioners choose a selective observation method, one or two of which we'll explore in a moment.

When you're doing an observation, it is important to make it clear to all the children that they are not to disturb you at all. You can explain to them that you're watching everybody and that you're writing down in your book all the brilliant things they're doing. It is very important not to name the target child or to make it obvious in any way that you're watching them. You can do this by moving your eyes and head as if you're looking at other children and then pretending to write a word or two. If your subject becomes involved in an incident of inappropriate behaviour during your observation session, resist the temptation to intervene. Leave it to one of your colleagues to sort out the situation, and use the chance to make a note of each of the child's reactions during this time. If you break off the observation to intervene, you could miss an example of behaviour or a piece of information that could be useful for the planning of the child's IEP.

Tracking observation

This method is good for observing the child in a 'free' situation, in other words when they're unsupported and left to select their activities. The observation will highlight which activities attract the child and for how long. You will need a floor plan of the setting and the observation consists of you tracking the child's movements between each activity area. This is done by drawing a line from area to area, with an arrow indicating the child's direction. When the child stays with an activity, you write the length of time they stayed there. Figure. 3.1 is an example of a completed tracking observation. You will see from this that Buster returned to the computer twice for longer periods of time than anywhere else, and also

| Figure 3.1 | An example of a completed tracking observation |

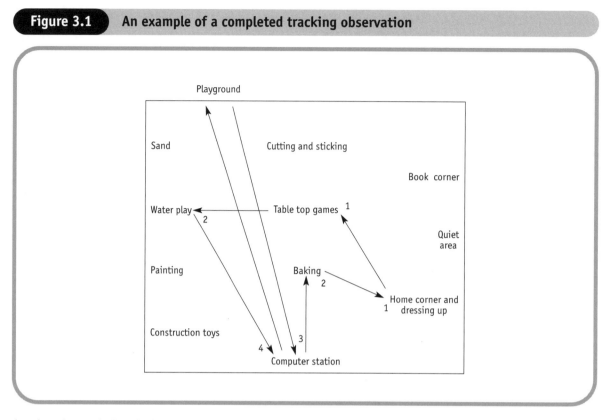

(Numbers denote the length of time in minutes spent at each activity)

that he didn't go to the book corner at all. His practitioner would need more examples to see whether this is a trend in Buster's free choice, but it may indicate his preferences and his dislikes. This is the sort of information that's important when deciding what will motivate Buster and what won't be very stimulating for him.

Spider's web observation

You can use this type of observation to check the child when they are doing activities that are supported by an adult. Ann Henderson (1994) explains how the spider's web observation helps to indicate whether the child can sustain in-depth play experiences.[3] This time the activities on offer are drawn around the edge of a circle. Again you track the child's movements between each activity area by drawing a line from area to area, an arrow indicating the direction of the child's movements. And again, you write the length of time the child stays with any activity. Figure 3.2 is an example of a completed spider's web observation. You will see this time that Buster went to the computer only once and again he didn't go to the book corner. Compared with the tracking observation, this one shows that Buster has spent slightly longer at each activity. It could be that he needs the support of his practitioner to focus his concentration on a task. This method of observation is also good for showing up Buster's likes and dislikes.

Figure 3.2 **An example of a completed spider's web observation**

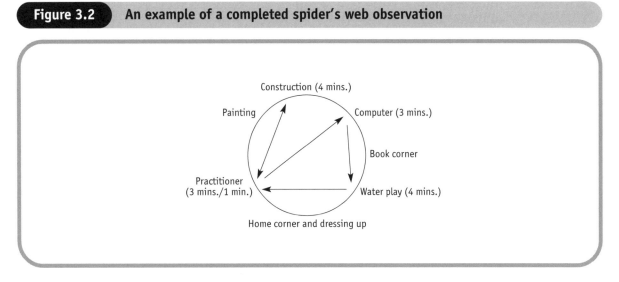

Buster Clayton; observed 18.4.2004; 9.15 – 9.30

Behavioural observation

This type of observation is very useful for identifying anything that may be influencing the child's behaviour, or for pinpointing what triggers bouts of inappropriate behaviour. You would usually conduct a behavioural observation using a chart designed to be used with the *ABC approach*. You will find a much fuller discussion of behavioural observations and the *ABC approach* in Chapter 4.

PLANNING AND WRITING IEPS: SOME GENERAL PRINCIPLES

Before we discuss what is involved in writing IEPs specifically for encouraging positive behaviour we need to think about some general points that will go a long way to making sure the IEP is well-planned, well-implemented and effective. These are points that you can keep in mind when you plan any type of IEP, and in time, it will be automatic for you to work this way.

- While the object of the IEP is to identify and support the areas that are giving the child difficulty, it is also very important to **celebrate the child's strengths**. Identifying where the child requires support must not be a long list of what Buster can't do but a brief description of where he's having difficulties. For example, *Buster has problems with working in small groups and also with sustaining attention for more than three minutes during structured sessions*. It can be easy to focus on the things that Buster can't do, but he will have strengths, talents and skills. You must identify these and use them as the point from which to work.

- To avoid overload, **work in small steps**. This is for both the child and yourself. You should choose targets relevant to both the child's needs and achievement level, and where you can, link them in with the relevant curriculum targets. Small increments of success will have more long-term consolidation. If you aim too high at first, your plan will probably fail in the end. If the child struggles to achieve a target, then you have set it too high. In that case, reduce the steps to even smaller ones and help the child to gradually work towards the original aim with success and confidence. Try to select targets that take the child from the point that they have already reached and have success with.

- The IEP isn't written in tablets of stone and can be **changed at any time**, as long as you discuss any changes with everybody involved. IEPs are flexible, working documents and if any of the elements in it seem to be failing the child, you must review and alter them accordingly. You don't have to wait until the official review if you need to change something: you can bring the meeting forward. You need to do this because the child's time is precious and they can't afford to lose any.

- Do you notice a **pattern emerging** in the results of the child's IEP? It could be in terms of *person, time, place* or *any combination* of these. For example, does Buster often or always fail to meet his targets in the same session? Have you checked whether there's a clash of personality between Buster and Mrs Smith, the practitioner who works with him? Is it because Buster does his IEP at 11.30 and Buster can smell lunch being made, which is hard on him if he hasn't had any breakfast? Is it because he works near the construction area and he's always being distracted by what is going on? If you do identify a problem, you must try to change whatever is the cause. So Buster could work with Mrs Jones instead, or at 9 o'clock after you've given him a drink and a couple of biscuits, or in the quiet corner instead.

- If the child seems to be struggling to achieve their targets, it could be that **the teaching methods** need to be reviewed. Again, this could involve person, place or time, but it could also be the choice of resources and equipment, the strategies you use, or the reward system you've chosen, or any combination of these. You should always use **positive** teaching methods. As we have already discussed, a child's self-esteem is tightly bound in with positive and confident interactions. It's stating the obvious to say that an unhappy child cannot learn effectively, but it is true, and the child who is experiencing behavioural difficulties needs both positive support and active encouragement.

- You should **involve the child and their parents** at every stage of the planning and operation of the IEP. They have an incentive to make it work if they've been involved, and it's also more likely to be meaningful to them. The child's age is not important since even very young children can be involved at an appropriate level, such as choosing from selected equipment or selecting an activity from several options.

- You should **review the child's progress** at least every three months. This is the time span recommended by the *Code of Practice*, but you should regard it as a minimum time span. As we have already seen, if the IEP seems to be failing the child for some reason, it is important to review it sooner rather than later.

- It's important that you **check previous achievements regularly**. You need to make sure that the child really has consolidated their earlier targets. It can easily happen in the 'busyness' of the setting for you to assume that Buster has retained a target he achieved three weeks ago, and that he can carry on to the next stages. The child can sometimes forget the skill or concept, and carrying on to the next stage will only end in failure. If Buster seems to have forgotten a target he previously achieved, then teach it to him again. If he hasn't retained a skill, then it's possible that somehow the original teaching may have been ineffective, so you should review this too and change it.

- Give the child **plenty of repetition**. They will need lots of practice to learn and consolidate a skill or concept, and you needn't be afraid of 'overkill'. As long as you put the concept across positively, in a fun way, with a variety of activities where appropriate, the child won't mind over-learning.

- While you would obviously praise the child whenever they achieve success, it's crucial that you also **praise them if they make a good effort**. Success breeds success and praise for achievement goes towards striving for even more achievement. But it's important to consciously praise effort as well, even if a target wasn't achieved. If Buster tried really hard during the session then you should tell him how pleased you are with his efforts. You must always be truthful, however, because the child will know if they didn't really achieve a target or didn't really try and if you praise them anyway, your praise will become valueless.

- If the child doesn't achieve a target during a session, **refer to their failure positively**. If they haven't managed to achieve a target, they don't want to have their disappointment reinforced by hearing you say things like, 'What a pity' or 'Oh dear, you didn't manage it today, did you, Buster?' If your comments on an unsuccessful outcome are positive, the child is less likely to become disheartened and give up trying. For example, saying something like 'Buster, you tried really hard today and you've almost hit your target. I bet you'll manage it tomorrow when we have another go. Well done!'

- You have to be prepared to **be flexible**. You might have to use lots of activities to put across a teaching point or to help the child to grasp a concept. This is where your imagination and ingenuity will come into its own. Some children can't generalize a point and you will have to re-teach it in other contexts. Doing this successfully means you need to be flexible in your approach.

- Another very important element to helping the child to achieve success is your ability to **be patient**. Practitioners are human and have problems and worries in their personal lives. Sometimes even the most patient person will be irritated by the child. If they and/or the session are winding you up, then simply stop the session and take time out to get back on an even keel. Some children know exactly which buttons to press if you're having an 'off day'. You won't gain anything by becoming stressed out, and neither will the child, so if it happens, it's best to leave things to calm down before trying again.

● It's very important for a child with behavioural difficulties that you are always **consistent**. They need stability and routine, and they're less likely to be confused if you provide a consistent approach. It's also useful if the child's main practitioner is absent and somebody else has to take over the programme, since they'll know what to do simply by following the notes on the IEP.

Let's move on from general principles now and explore what's involved in the actual writing of IEPs.

● The IEP form

Most Local Education Authorities (LEAs) have their own version of an IEP form, but the basic ingredients of any IEP *pro forma* will be the same, regardless of where the child lives. This standardisation was brought about by the first *SEN Code of Practice*, to ensure that the child's records could be passed on and easily assimilated in a new authority's system when they moved between areas or changed LEAs.

IEP forms must include four basic elements:

i The area(s) of concern. In other words, the reasons *why* an IEP is to be implemented. As we have already discussed, you need to highlight the area(s) of concern to give a focus to the IEP and to enable effective planning. It follows then that the selected targets really will address the child's areas of need.

ii The targets to be reached, with criteria for success. In other words, *what* will be the child's specific aims, agreed by everybody involved in planning the IEP. The targets for a child with behavioural difficulties should be tied in with both the positive behaviour policy and the moral values of the setting. By making these connections, you will be able to identify exactly which of the setting's rules are being challenged by the child and then you can plan appropriately.

iii The strategies to be used. In other words *how* the IEP will be followed. The strategies outline what methods you have agreed to implement the IEP to enable the child to achieve their targets.

iv The review of the plan. In other words *when* the IEP will be looked at again, and discussed in regard to its effectiveness. This review takes place at an agreed time, usually three months after the start of the programme, although, as we have seen, you can bring this forward if necessary. The aim of the review is to assess whether the child has achieved the targets within the allotted time span, and to decide what further action to take, if any.

As well as these pieces of information, IEP forms should also include the following:

i   The child's areas of strength. This gives an important and positive focus for the abilities and achievements of the child as well as an indication of the point from which you should begin the targets.

ii   The staff involved. Naming the practitioner(s) who will be doing the IEP with the child helps to give it structure, consistency and stability. Everybody connected with the child knows who is involved; outside agents can see who is involved; and it shows who was involved if the IEP is sent to the LEA as part of the evidence for statutory assessment.

iii The frequency of the programme. This piece of information also adds structure and routine to the IEP, and everybody involved knows when it is being used. For example *Ten minutes every morning or Monday, Wednesday and Friday lunchtime*. If the child is referred for statutory assessment, this record shows how often you implemented the programme.

iv   The equipment or apparatus used, if relevant. Including this information helps you to save time because you can get out what is needed for a session by reading the IEP; it highlights which resources are very successful with the child and conversely those that fail to excite or interest the child; shows a substitute practitioner what needs to be used, if you are absent; and provides a record for outside agents of what resources you have used, thereby helping them to suggest alternatives.

You will find a photocopiable blank IEP form at the end of the chapter on page 68.

Writing the IEP

The *SEN Code of Practice* recommends that you focus on a maximum of three or four targets, and you should focus on the area(s) causing most concern. Since the *Code of Practice* says a *maximum* of three or four, you have a bit of flexibility. If for example the child can manage most effectively with only two targets, then select only two. For some children working on a behaviour IEP, even one target could be enough. When deciding on the number of targets, you could use the analogy of the speed limit on the motorway: you don't *have* to drive at the maximum of 70 miles per hour; if you feel comfortable travelling at the top speed then that's fine, but nobody is making you put your foot down and zoom along if you're not confident in doing so. When you plan the IEP, if you do go for only one or two targets, make a note about this on the form as a record of your professional judgement. The targets you choose should be **SMART**, that is: **S**pecific, **M**easurable, **A**chievable, **R**elevant and **T**ime-related.

● Ask the child's parents for their input since they are the experts in their own child. They can give you useful tips and suggestions, making an important contribution to the planning. By involving the parents you're sending out an important signal that you value and respect their contribution. It helps you to forge a positive mutual relationship with them and it helps them to feel that they are actively supporting their child.

● Write the targets concisely. The term used in the *Code of Practice* is 'crisp'. Try to avoid jargon or flowery language, and write the targets in clear, specific terms that can be followed and understood by anybody reading the IEP.

● Together, agree on the criteria for success. In other words, you need to decide how everybody involved will know when the child has achieved the target. The criteria must be specific and clear, without any room for confusion. For example, if Buster is trying to avoid getting into fights during playtimes, the criterion for success could be *Buster will have five minutes positive playtime every morning for one week*. The following week, his target might be increased to eight minutes, or decreased to four minutes depending on whether and how easily he achieved his target.

● Together, agree on methods you will use to acknowledge and celebrate the child's success. You will need to use your judgement here because the reward must be meaningful for the child. For example, putting their own stickers on a chart, being allowed an extra session at the computer, being able to choose any activity they want. You must be very careful not to use a 'play' session as a reward, since you may create in the child's mind a distinction between 'work' and 'play'.

● Keep detailed records of the child's progress since they provide vital evidence of the child's achievements particularly over a longer period of time. In the 'busyness' of the setting, you can easily become disheartened and think that the child isn't progressing. When you look back at earlier targets though, you'll be able to see just how much progress the child has made. However, if the child is among the minority who have to go forward for statutory assessment, these records are crucial for the body of evidence which you will be asked for by the LEA.

WRITING A POSITIVE BEHAVIOUR IEP

Once you decide to plan a positive behaviour plan, it's crucial that you help the child to realise that it's their *behaviour* which you will not tolerate, and not the child themselves. Through supporting the child you can show them that you're all working together to help them develop acceptable and appropriate behaviour.

When you decide to plan a programme for the child, you can boil it down to two fundamental questions: 'What exactly is the behaviour we want to alter?' and 'How are we going to alter it?'

- Try to be specific about the behaviour which you find unacceptable. Use precise language. 'Buster's quite unkind to the other children' doesn't tell us much; 'Buster pinches other children during circle time' does.

- Having identified what you want to change about the child's behaviour, go on to the next stage and be specific about the positive behaviour you're aiming for. 'Buster will sit in circle time and keep control of his hands' is more focused than 'Buster will develop more social behaviour during circle time'.

- Add a time element to your plan. For example, are you aiming for Buster to have positive circle time every day, three days a week or once every five days? Only you will know the parameters because it depends on the child and their needs, abilities and achievement level, and the seriousness of the difficulty.

- After identifying the behaviour you want to change, look for its opposite positive behaviour and then model it and teach it. For example, if the child throws toys around, say 'If you throw the toys and they hit Megan she'll be hurt, Buster. I'll help you to put them carefully back into the box' or 'If you tear those books we won't have many left for story time so we'll look after them. Please bring me the pieces and I'll stick them back in the book'. Watch for even the smallest example of positive behaviour and praise the child for it. Praise other children for positive behaviours. 'That was kind, Buster, to help Tanya with her coat' or 'Well done, José for closing the door quietly – did you see that, everybody?'

- The language you use should be positive and calm. It's understandable that when you're very busy with a group of children and you spot Buster destroying your most recent table display, your immediate reaction is to shout across the room, 'Buster stop it – you mustn't do that!' It will be more effective if you can handle it another way. For example, go across to Buster and sort out the situation in a calm, quiet and positive manner; if you can't leave the group, signal to another adult to see to Buster; if you'd prefer to deal with Buster yourself, get another adult to take your group; or invite Buster to join your group and do the exciting activity on offer and go back later with him to encourage and help him sort out the messed up display.

- If you ever issue a 'If you do xxx, then xxx will happen' warning, be sure that you carry out the sanction. You can often hear an adult in the street say to a child, 'You do that again and I'll take you home', followed a few moments later by, 'I'm warning you . . .', and then 'I will – I'll take you home' (or even worse threats). And as they move off down the street, the child is still doing whatever it was and the adult is still threatening. The threats become meaningless because they're not carried out, so the child never learns that their inappropriate behaviour brings with it a real sanction.

- When you begin to put your IEP into action you may experience a worsening of the child's behaviour in the early stages. It's very important not to become disheartened if this happens. Some children may find it difficult to handle the 'regime' imposed by the IEP and react in the only way they know. This is particularly so for those children whose inappropriate behaviour is primarily attention seeking. Don't give up on the IEP, or lose self-confidence in your own abilities to carry it through successfully. The child may be just testing how far they can 'push' things over the mark. If you do feel a little uneasy, make sure you get support and reassurance from the other members of the team.

- Sometimes things don't work out quite as you'd planned them and you'll need to ask yourself why. Go back to the general principles of working with IEPs that we discussed earlier and see whether any of the elements of person, place and time might be at the root of poor progress. Maybe the rewards and incentives aren't very appealing to the child, so a change there might do the trick. Check whether your approach could be more attractive for the child: Is it interesting? Is it consistent? Is it practical enough? Is it giving the child enough time to really absorb the skills and/or behaviour you're working on? Is it clear to the child what you want of them? Are you giving the child enough positive attention? And the final question, do you think you need to ask for specialised advice? In other words, a move to *Early Years Action Plus*.

There's an example on page 55 of a completed positive behaviour IEP for Buster.

You'll notice that Buster's practitioner has focused on his strengths to give a starting point for implementing the IEP, while the areas of concern are described in clear and specific terms. Buster's targets and criteria for success outline exactly what it is hoped Buster will achieve, how, when and where. This clarity also helps Buster to know exactly what is expected of him. By stating when the targets should be achieved, the practitioner is setting a deadline by which to gauge whether the targets and/or criteria are appropriate, and if not, to change them without wasting too much of Buster's time. The strategy for Buster's first target uses his enjoyment of construction toys as a reward system for achieving his targets, while the second one exploits his pleasure in the computer and his ability to concentrate on it, as a reward for achieving his target. The date of the review ties in with the date set for Buster to achieve his targets, so there's no time lag between the two.

Figure 3.3	An example of a completed positive behaviour IEP

Child's name: Buster Clayton   **DOB:** 13.2.2000

Date IEP implemented: 31.3.04   **C of P level:** EY Action

Areas of strength: Buster enjoys the computer: he will work on it for up to 10 minutes; he's interested in construction toys.

Areas of concern: 1 Buster shouts out during group activities.
2 Buster runs around the room during structured activity time.

Targets and criteria for success: 1 Buster will wait quietly for his turn to speak during group activities of five minutes, initially for two mornings per week, increasing to five mornings per week.
2 Buster will concentrate on a structured activity, initially for two minutes, three days per week, rising to five minutes five days per week.

Targets to be reached by: 1 30.6.04
2 30.6.04

Strategies to be used: 1 Buster can put a sticker on his achievement chart each time he waits quietly during group activities. Five stickers mean he can play with the construction toys for an extra session.
2 Buster will be allowed an extra 5 minutes on the computer each time he achieves his target for structured activities.

Adults involved: Mrs Jones will work with Buster in nursery, Buster's Mum will use a Play plan at home.

Resources/equipment: Activities as appropriate; Buster's achievement chart and stickers, Play plan for home.

Date of next review: 30.6.04

Parent's/carer's comment: I'll do what I can to help Buster.

Practitioner's signature: *Mary Bloggs* **(SENCO)**

CASE STUDY

Lucy is 4 years old. She has only just started nursery because her mother preferred to keep her at home, until she thought Lucy was old enough to cope with all the other children. The childcare practitioner, Pearl, is already worried about Lucy because she plays on her own and often just watches the other children from the side lines. Indeed, she is so quiet that Pearl often forgets that she is there and this makes her feel very guilty. Lucy speaks very quietly and Pearl has noticed other nursery workers getting very impatient with the child. The other children and some of the adults are showing that they are irritated by Lucy when she refuses to join in group activities or to try new experiences. One of the nursery workers confides in Pearl that she resents all the one-to-one attention that Lucy is getting because it is taking the adults away from the other children. The other children are beginning to pick on Lucy and the staff are getting frustrated. Lucy's mother looks unhappy but has not said anything to the staff, leaving the nursery as quickly as she can after dropping off Lucy or picking her up.

(Source: *Understanding Children's Challenging Behaviour*, Penny Mukherji, [Nelson Thornes, 2001])

Using the positive behaviour IEP form on page 68 try to decide on a plan of action for Lucy. There's a suggested plan on page 66 at the end of the chapter.

WORKING WITH THE CHILD AND THEIR PARENTS IN PLANNING IEPS

Close involvement of the child and their parents is crucial for the IEP's success. A 'home-grown' IEP (one which has had the input of the child's people) is more likely to have in it meaningful and stimulating plans, and their vested interest means they have more incentive to make it work. It gives the child a sense of the 'team spirit' in working together to support them.

The child

- Speak to the child about their difficulties. Without going into detail help the child realise that there are some things that they may need support with. Do this in an atmosphere of 'we're all special in our own way; we're all good at some things; we all need help with some things'.

- Explain clearly why you're planning an IEP. Talk about how the child's parents and everybody in the setting will decide how to help them to carry on making progress. Understanding that everybody is working together to help them gives the child confidence in knowing that they're being supported. Realising that they're very much part of the team, their involvement becomes very real and very important to them.

- Make sure that the child understands the goals and targets of their IEP. If they see what it's all about they'll be happier at being involved and they'll be motivated.

- Explain why individual support is needed for the child, for example a learning support assistant. Talk about what it is that makes the child need help, and how the LSA is there to help them make progress.

- Be sensitive to the potential stress and anxiety that planning the IEP and follow up reviews may cause the child. The child may develop anxieties simply by not knowing or understanding what's going on. Watch for any signs of this and talk calmly and positively to the child about what it's all about.

- If you need to involve outside agents, make sure the child understands their role. It might scare the child when 'outsiders' become involved so try to alleviate any anxieties. Explain that these people have been specially trained to help children with the same type of difficulties as themselves. If possible, persuade the people from outside agencies who are linked with your setting to be there occasionally, so the children get used to them. If this could be at drop-off or collection time so that the parents can get to meet them too, then all the better. It reduces the perception of 'them' being 'brought in'.

- Find out about advocacy services for children or pupil support services that are available locally. If the child's parents (or sometimes the children themselves) feel isolated or in need of more support these services can help.

- Allocate a key member of staff to the child. A vital part of this support for the child is knowing there's one adult they can go to.

- If the child is already involved with an outside agency, explain to them that you will all be working together to support them. The child may think that the other professionals belong to 'the other place', for example at home or in the clinic. Explain that the other adults will still be helping them, but that now everybody in the setting will be part of the team.

- If the child is 'looked after' by the local authority, establish a positive and cooperative relationship with the carers. It's just as crucial for the 'looked after' child to see that foster parents or house parents are involved as it is for a child from a conventional background. Explain that their foster parents care for them and are an important part of the team too.

- If you think it will work, establish a 'buddy' system or 'circle of friends' to give peer support to the child. The child's peer group is a very valuable resource that we often overlook. The other children can be wonderful as role models, supporters, encouragers, demonstrators or correctors. If you have a group of children who can do these things, then tap that bank of skills!

⬤ The parents

To gain the parents' confidence, you must develop an awareness of their needs, especially if for some reason they aren't able to communicate these needs themselves. For example, they may have learning difficulties, they may have a communication disorder, or they may have only recently become aware of their child's difficulties and are going through the first stages of coming to terms with the problem.

It's important you approach the issue by saying something like 'We feel Buster finds it very hard to sit still during story time. How do you find him at home?' rather than 'We feel Buster's got a behaviour problem. Is he a pain with you too?'

Emotional and behavioural difficulties are regarded as special educational needs, and the child who is experiencing these, and the parents of that child have the right to access any support and help offered by the local education authority. So make sure the parents are informed about the local Parent Partnership Service (PPS).

Work on joint initiatives with the parents, 'joint initiatives' being anything from a Play plan developed between yourselves, the child and the parents, to a project linking up with another setting or school for shared activities. It has been known for parents to organise these through their own contacts.

Play plans are excellent for offering the parents a way of positively supporting their child, that reinforces and practises what the child is doing in the setting and reassures the parents that they're actually *doing* something towards their child's progress. Figure 3.4 on page 59 shows an example of a Play plan and you'll find a blank photocopiable Play plan form at the end of the chapter on page 70.

If the parents have only recently been told of their child's difficulties, they might be feeling bewildered, alone or even be going through a grieving process. Even if there were difficulties with the child at home, the parents may have thought the child would come through a short period of 'just being naughty', and when a professional raises the issue, it may be a shock.

Be prepared for a variety of reactions by the parents. Coming to terms with a difficulty is a process unique to each parent. They may experience disbelief, denial, grief, self-blame, even aggression. They may also react with 'Thank goodness someone else believes me and has given it a name!' If the child has been diagnosed as having Attention Deficit Disorder (ADD) or Attention Deficit Hyperactivity Disorder (AD/HD), their parents will need your sensitive support.

If the parents don't speak English as their first language, they may need support from somebody within their community in terms of translation and even in terms of moral support. Make sure that any translation offered is of a high quality – sometimes misunderstandings can occur because a 'the' or 'a' has been left out of translation.

Figure 3.4 **An example of a Play plan for home/setting liaison**

Play Plan for <u>Buster Clayton</u> and <u>Buster's family</u>

<u>Buster</u> will play these games to help <u>increase his concentration span and to take his turn</u>.

1 Buster chooses a toy or game (not the computer) and plays positively with it together with brother Toby for five minutes, then increasing by a minute each time he reaches his target. When Buster reaches a target, he can play alone on the computer for the same length of time or more if he wants.

2 Buster, Toby, Mum and Dad take turns to choose a board game. Buster takes his turns during the game. Let Buster keep the record of who chose the game by sticking the smiley faces on the chart next to each person's name, every night.

<u>Begin by</u>

(for target 1) giving Buster a maximum of two games to choose from. You can increase the number of games when he's ready for bigger choices. If five minutes is too long for Buster to play positively with Toby, reduce it to four or three. Let him have the session on the computer as soon as he reaches his target.

(for target 2) giving free choice of game to whoever has the turn that night. Buster fills in the record chart. Have fun playing the game, encouraging Buster to take his turn properly. Stop the game straight away if Buster refuses to wait his turn and explain why. (Don't let him play on the computer afterwards if this happens.)
If Buster's tired or fed up during any of the game sessions, finish them quickly on a happy and enjoyable note.

Here's what <u>Buster</u> did:

Continued

Monday 5 April. Buster chose Connect Four and played with Toby for four minutes before having a wobbly. I stopped the game and he didn't have his Game Boy on. We played Happy Families in the evening (Dad's choice – I think he's trying to tell me something!) and Buster was great.

Tuesday 6 April. Buster chose Connect Four again. He played well with Toby for five minutes and 35 seconds. He then played on the computer for about ten minutes. I chose Ludo. Buster wouldn't wait for his turn so we packed up the game.

Wednesday 7 April. Today was great. Buster and Toby played with their Lego for about ten minutes with no fights. I let him play on the computer till teatime.

Buster chose snakes and ladders and he waited his turn every time. He didn't want the computer again, so he watched a bit of telly instead.

Thursday 8 April. Buster was a bit narky today and only lasted seven minutes with Toby on the Jackstraws. But I let him go on the computer because he got more than his five minutes target. Toby chose Jackstraws again for the family game and Buster went ballistic so I put the game away and he didn't have computer. I think he was tired.

Friday 9 April – couldn't do the programme because we had to take the boys to swimming and football practice.

Saturday 10 April. Buster was brilliant today. He played with Toby in the garden for about 15 minutes taking turns on the swing and climbing frame. He had about ten minutes on the computer. Dad chose Kerplonk and we had a great time. Buster took his turn and didn't lose his rag.

Sunday 11 April. We went to Grandma's and Buster and Toby played with Grandad's old Meccano set. They were at it for about half an hour and no fights. (Heaven!) Buster didn't want the computer when we got home so we all played Jackstraws. I chose it to see what would happen after Thursday night, but it was great. We played for about 15 minutes.

Buster and Toby usually play their game while I cook the tea. We play the family games in the evening before bedtime. I think it's beginning to sink in with Buster.

Date when this Play plan was finished at home: <u>Sunday 11 April 2004</u>

Some parents have disabilities or difficulties themselves and you'll need to offer help and support where you can, without being patronising. The parents' personal experience of special needs education may have been bad and if so, you may have a few barriers to break down. If they have an alternative communication system, take time to learn it, especially if the child uses it as well.

OTHER PEOPLE WHO MAY BE INVOLVED

We've explored the issues involved in making sure the child and their parents are fully active in planning and writing the IEP, but they're only a part of the team, albeit the core. You need to include the rest of the people involved with the setting, such as the other practitioners, lunchtime supervisors, outside agents if applicable, other adults such as parents or visitors, and so on. Only some of these people would be actively involved in the planning of the IEP, but all of them should be involved in the implementation of your positive behaviour policy in general, and the aims of the IEP in particular.

As we have already seen, the child needs consistency and stability, and encouraging 'outside' adults who visit the setting to adopt your attitudes and approaches will ensure that the child gets seamless support. For example, it isn't any use adopting a certain approach to Buster and not sharing this with the local grandma who comes into the setting to do baking with the children, because by her own perceptions, attitudes and practices, she may unwittingly undermine what you're trying to do.

If you've asked a specialist agent for help, you can focus more specifically on methods and strategies recommended by them that are likely to have a positive affect on the child's development, learning and behaviour. Sharing this expertise with everybody in the setting means the child gets a network of consistent support. The parents and the child must be involved in liaison with outside agents. Naturally, they won't be expected to have the same specialist knowledge, but they do have their own expertise to offer. For example, the intimate knowledge the parents have of their child means they'll be able to advise whether a suggested method of incentive-and-reward will work; through the child's own self-knowledge they'll be able to say whether a target is attractive, whether the rewards are motivating and whether the activities are exciting.

REVIEWING AN IEP

So, you've put Buster's IEP into place and after three months (or less if appropriate) it's time to review it. How do you go about this?

- Set up a system of trigger-reminders in your diary, working backwards from the review date. Start about four weeks before the date of the review, like this:

| Figure 3.5 | Termly IEP Review Planner |

28.05.04 – Buster Clayton's review due on 30.06.04 – request information and advice from:

Mr and Mrs Clayton (parents), Mrs Jones (EY teacher), Mrs Bloggs (SENCO), Mrs Harris (Social Worker)

NB – advice to be received here by *11.06.04*

7.06.04 – advice received so far from Mrs Jones and Mrs Bloggs

NB – remind parents and Mrs Harris advice due 11 June

11.06.04 – has everybody sent advice? Chase missing documents

16.06.04 – send invitations and advice documentation for Buster Clayton's review

29.06.04 – get coffee, biscuits and flowers for Buster Clayton's review

30.06.04 – Buster Clayton's review: 10.00 a.m.

- Make the room cheerful and welcoming. Coffee and biscuits and some flowers on the table have an amazing effect. If you can, invite the parents to come a few minutes earlier and help them relax. If English isn't their first language they may need an interpreter, so don't forget to arrange (a good) one.

- Put the chairs in a circle to reduce the 'them and us' feel and emphasise the team approach.

- Refer to the Review Form and work your way through it systematically. This helps to keep everybody focused on the point under discussion.

- Invite the main practitioner for their input. This is crucial as they're working most closely with the child.

- Invite the other agents for their contribution. If somebody has sent in a report because they can't attend the meeting, read out their comments.

- Make sure that the child's parents (and the child if appropriate) get a chance to express their opinion. It's vital that they feel confident enough to make a contribution and that they aren't intimidated.

- Give time for everybody to express their opinions, watching out for those people aiming for a *Bafta* award! As Chair, you can interrupt the long monologues of those who hog the limelight and so give the other people a chance.

- Have a section on the form for a plan of further action. You can cut this down to a simple yes/no deletion system.

- Before finishing, summarise briefly what was said and what action was decided upon. Check if everybody agrees with your summary. This is very important to avoid any complaints later on.

- Book the date of the next review – people's diaries fill up very quickly so while you have everybody there, book them in.

- Sign and date the Review Form. If you can, give the parents a copy immediately, otherwise as soon as possible. If you can, try to have a quiet word with them to make sure they are happy with the outcome of the review. This is especially important for parents who are shy, or who feel upset or threatened by the whole thing.

- Copy the Review Form and circulate it to everybody who attended the review as soon as possible. Make two or three extra copies and keep them on file because *somebody* is bound to ring you up saying, 'I've lost my copy . . .'

Figure 3.6 shows an example of a completed IEP Review Form, and you will find a blank, photocopiable form on page 69.

Figure 3.6   **An example of a completed Positive Behaviour IEP Review Form**

Positive Behaviour IEP Review Form

Child's name: Buster Clayton   DOB: 13.2.2000

Level: Early Years Action/~~Early Years Action Plus~~ [delete as appropriate]

Date of review: 30.06.2004   1st/~~2nd~~/~~3rd~~ review [delete as appropriate]

Present at review: Mrs Clayton (mother), Mrs Jones (EY teacher), Mrs Bloggs (SENCO)

Reports of child's progress /IEP:

Mrs Jones:

1 Buster has made progress and now waits quietly for his turn to speak during group activities. He's now up to four minutes, and sometimes longer every morning. I've found that giving the children a wooden egg to hold while it's their turn to speak helps Buster.

2 Buster's a bit slower with this target but he's coming on. He's managing about three minutes or so, most days. By always having the next activity ready, I'm able to forestall any bouts of inappropriate behaviour I see building up, by immediately distracting him.

Mrs Clayton:
We're still following Play plans at home and Buster's doing well with them.

We're all enjoying spending time together as a family and I'm sure it's helping Buster with his behaviour. He doesn't fight with Toby so much now. I'm pleased with what you're doing for him.

Additional comments/reports from people not present:

a)

b)

Continued

c)

Further action: Continue with IEP? Yes / ~~No~~   Modify IEP? ~~Yes~~ / No

Remain at present stage?   Yes / ~~No~~   Move to next stage? ~~Yes~~ / No

Discontinue SEN procedure?   ~~Yes~~ / No   Other action? ~~Yes~~ / No

Next review due: 28 September 2004

Signed: *Josephine Bloggs* (SENCO)   Date: **30 June 2004**

SUMMARY

In this chapter we explored aspects of writing and implementing positive behaviour IEPs by

- looking at ways of identifying and recording inappropriate behaviour particularly through observations;

- examining some general principles behind the planning and writing of IEPs;

- exploring the practicalities involved in writing IEPs specifically for children with behavioural difficulties;

- discussing the holistic approach to planning IEPs;

- exploring working with the child and their parents to ensure their involvement in the planning and implementation of the IEP;

- looking at the practicalities involved in conducting reviews of IEPs.

| **Figure 3.7** | **A suggested Positive Behaviour IEP for Lucy** |

Child's name: Lucy Jenson   **DOB:** 14. 8. 2000

Date IEP implemented: 18.4.04   **C of P level:** EY Action

Areas of strength: Lucy can concentrate well; Lucy can be determined

Areas of concern: Undeveloped social skills; poor communication skills; lack of confidence to try new experiences

Targets and criteria for success: 1 Lucy will do a familiar activity with an adult and one other child, increasing to three more children, for five minutes, increasing to ten minutes, every morning.
2 Lucy will share a favourite book with an adult once per week, increasing to five times per week
3 Lucy will choose and try a new activity with adult support once per week, increasing to five times per week.

Targets to be reached by: 16.7.2004

Strategies used: A key worker will be allocated to Lucy, responsible for helping Lucy to achieve her targets. Lucy will get a sticker for each target achieved; five stickers will earn her a free choice of activity, alone if she wishes.

Adults involved: Mrs Ryan will work with Lucy in the nursery. Lucy's Mum will follow a Play plan at home.

Resources/equipment: Activities as appropriate, stickers, Play plan for home.

Date of next review: 16.7.2004

Parent's/carer's comment: *I want to help Lucy all I can and I will do the Play plan at home.*

Practitioner's signature: *Mary Ryan*

Lucy's ability to concentrate is shown when she spends time watching the other children; her resistance to joining in, or to try new experiences shows she can be determined. These characteristics can be good when working towards her targets. The targets are written in specific terms, so Lucy knows exactly what she's aiming for.

The practitioners realised that Lucy's intensive shyness means she finds difficulty in coping with too many different people. She will gain the confidence she needs to develop her social skills from the support of the allocated key worker.

References

1 and 2 *Developing Individual Behaviour Plans in Early Years*, Hannah Mortimer (NASEN, 2000).

3 *Observation and Record Keeping*, Ann Henderson (Pre-school Learning Alliance, 1994).

Positive Behaviour Individual Education Plan

Child's name: DOB:

Date IEP implemented: C of P level:

Areas of strength:

Areas of concern:

Targets and criteria for success:

Targets to be reached by:

Strategies to be used:

Adults involved:

Resources/equipment:

Date of next review:

Parent's/carer's comments:

Practitioner's signature:

Positive Behaviour IEP Review Form

Child's name: DOB:

Level: Early Years Action/Early Years Action Plus [delete as appropriate]

Date of review: 1st/2nd/3rd review [delete as appropriate]

Present at review:

Reports of child's progress/IEP:

Additional comments/reports from people not present:

a)

b)

c)

Further action: Continue with IEP? Yes/No   Modify IEP? Yes/No

Remain at present stage?   Yes/No   Move to next stage? Yes/No

Discontinue SEN procedure?   Yes/No   Other action? Yes/No

Next review due:

Signed: Date:

Play plan

Play plan for _____ and _____ will

_____ play these games to help _____

_____ :

Begin by

Here's what _____ did:

Date when this Play plan was finished at home: _____

Chapter 4

How to reduce inappropriate behaviours while encouraging positive ones

(Or: Wait-watchers – the way forward)

This chapter will explore strategies for both reducing inappropriate behaviour and encouraging positive behaviour by

- examining the *ABC approach*, so looking at behaviour management in terms of *cause and effect*, and how this can help you to plan ways of supporting the child;

- exploring some ways of *observing and identifying* inappropriate behaviour, so enabling you to gather information you can use to put effective strategies into place;

- suggesting positive and effective interventions, including some *general principles* behind managing challenging behaviour in the setting, and also some more *specific strategies* so helping you to encourage positive behaviour in the child;

- using case studies as a means of planning some possible strategies for effective support.

If you've been tempted to turn to this chapter first, you may find it a good idea to read Chapter 2 first. Developing good practice in working with children who have special needs follows a logical process, including the importance for us as practitioners to 'peel back the layers' of comfort and complacency that build up over our years of experience. There are some hard-hitting questions in Chapter 2 that we all need to ask ourselves and answer honestly before we can expect to support a child in their progress. If you haven't already done your self-scrutiny exercise, what follows in this chapter will have less effect than if you have.

When a child persistently displays inappropriate behaviour, it is quite understandable that, as the practitioner dealing at first hand with the problems, you want a quick fix or that you may feel pressurised to sort out the difficulties immediately. If you can step back from this reaction and become a 'wait-watcher', the long-term results will pay off.

The phrase 'wait-watcher' means exactly that: wait – be patient and take as much time as you need to build up an overview of the child, their behaviour in different situations and their reactions to certain stimuli; and watch – carry out your observations carefully and do as many of them as you think necessary to furnish you with the information you need to effectively plan the way forward for the child, you and everybody involved.

There is no single strategy or technique that you can use for all children, because each child is unique and will react to different methods in his or her own way. However, there are plenty of tried and true techniques that work well. The more ideas you have at your disposal to try, the more likely you are to hit on the strategy that works for any particular child.

BEHAVIOUR MANAGEMENT THEORY (OR 'CAUSE AND EFFECT')

The main principle behind behaviour management theory is that if we perform an action and have a *pleasant* experience as a result, we are more likely to repeat that action. The pleasant experience is called a *reward* and this is likely to make us *increase* our performance of the original action. For example, a baby might throw her rattle out of her pram and her mum picks it up, shakes it while smiling and cooing, then returns it. The baby enjoys this interaction so throws the rattle out again in the hope that Mum will play the game once more. On an adult level, if we buy a certain chocolate bar that we find delicious, we are likely to buy that one again the next time we want to eat chocolate.

On the other hand, if we do something and we have an *unpleasant* experience as a result, we are less likely to do that thing again. The unpleasant reaction is called a *sanction* (or sometimes you may see it referred to as a *punishment*) and is likely to make us *decrease* the original behaviour or action. So the baby who throws out the rattle is less likely to repeat the action if her mum's immediate reaction is to become irritated with the child and harshly tell her to stop throwing her rattle out of her pram. If we buy a certain chocolate bar and find we have bad stomach ache and feelings of nausea afterwards, we are more likely to choose something else next time we fancy eating sweets.

A sanction isn't always an *active application* of an unpleasant experience – it can also be the deprivation of a reward. So, for example, if Buster has a temper tantrum because his mum won't buy him the latest 'gotta-have' toy, (and Mum really does stick to her decision!), he will learn that his behaviour does not get him his reward (i.e. the toy), so he is less likely to repeat the temper tantrum. The sanction or 'punishment' is the deprivation of Buster's desire.

This theory of behaviour management can be applied in any context, and you can use it to plan and put into practice strategies that support the child and help them develop positive behaviour skills.

THE *ABC APPROACH*

The 'ABC' of this technique stands for **A**ntecedent, **B**ehaviour and **C**onsequence. The approach itself comprises a four-step process that gathers information about the child and the context in which they display unacceptable behaviour, in order to plan a strategy to reduce the likelihood of the behaviour recurring.

The **antecedent** means the situation or event that leads up to the inappropriate behaviour; the **behaviour** is what the child does that is unacceptable; and the **consequence** is what occurs immediately afterwards as a result of the child's behaviour.

A crucial component of the *ABC approach* is good quality observations. Fortunately, observation is now a fundamental and official part of the identification and assessment process at the Foundation stage, since the DfES recognises its value. Early years practitioners have been making observations of children since Adam was a lad, and already know the vital part they play in building up an overall picture of a child's development, so doing them as part of the *ABC approach* will be nothing new.

The four-step process of the *ABC approach*:

Step 1. The first step is to make **observations** that will provide information about the **A**ntecedent to the behaviour (i.e. the situation or event leading up to the behaviour), the **B**ehaviour itself (i.e. a clear description of what the child does), and the **C**onsequences (i.e. what happened as a result). These observations should record carefully and accurately each stage of the process, and you should do as many as you need to build up a picture of the child's behaviour. This will help you to pinpoint any possible situations that may be responsible for triggering the inappropriate behaviour in the child.

An example of an *ABC approach* observation might be

Buster and Melanie were making models of trains, using junk and boxes for their own model. (This is the antecedent, setting the scene and giving the context in which the children are working.)

Buster told Melanie that he wanted the box she was holding and he pinched her arm with the nails of his thumb and forefinger. He then snatched the box from Melanie's hand. (This is the behaviour – an exact description of what Buster did.)

Melanie screamed and ran to Mrs Davies, who took the box from Buster and told him to leave the workshop. (This is a description of the consequence – what happened afterwards as a result of Buster's behaviour.)

You will find an example of a completed form (Figure 4.1) on page 90 and a photocopiable form you can use for recording observations as part of the *ABC approach* (Figure 4.2) on page 91.

Step 2. After you have made your observations, the next stage is the **selection** of the behaviour you want to discourage. Try not to overload yourself or the child at the initial stages of planning how you are going to work together. You will have to ignore some of the less urgent but still unacceptable behaviours, and plan how to tackle those later on. At first, it is best to choose just one or two behaviours to work on. Choose the one that is causing the most disruption or the one that is going to be the easiest to change. You may find that discussing this with the child's parents and your colleagues will help, since they could have observed behaviours that you are not yet aware of, but that are more pressing than those you have seen yourself.

Step 3. The third step in the approach is the **identification** of what causes the behaviour you are wishing to change. Again, through discussions with the child's parents and your colleagues, decide together what seems to be making the child repeat the undesired behaviour. For example, by pinching the other children, Buster eventually gets from them what he wants; another child may have apparently uncontrollable behaviour as a result of confusion about changes in the activities, or even some of the displays on the walls. When you think you have identified a possible cause, use this information to draw up a plan to effect change.

Step 4. The final step in the process is the **application** of a plan that will change the **A** (the antecedents), the **B** (the behaviour) and therefore the **C** (the consequences).

Changing the antecedents will help to reduce the possibility of triggering the inappropriate behaviour. For example, avoid putting the child in situations that are likely to spark off the behaviour; give them lots of positive attention before the behaviour occurs, so pre-empting any displays; or have ready a few enjoyable and interesting things to do so that you can occupy the child during 'dead' times between activities and avoid allowing boredom to set in, which could result in inappropriate behaviour.

Changing the behaviour will help the child to realise that what they do is not the way they are going to achieve their goal. You can help to change the child's behaviour by, for example, praising the child for a positive behaviour which is incompatible with the undesired one; showing the child a different behaviour which is opposite to the undesired one, either by modelling it yourself or by praising another child who does something along the lines that you're aiming for; or trying to stop the undesired behaviour *as soon as it seems to be starting*, by offering a distraction or by removing the child from the situation.

Changing the consequences will help the child to realise that appropriate behaviour is much more pleasant and will result in them achieving their goal or reward. For example, use your knowledge of what the child enjoys to teach them that behaving appropriately can be fun and rewarding; reward them for not behaving inappropriately, again using the things that they like or enjoy as the means to do this; and make sure you are always consistent in demanding what is required of them.

OBSERVATIONS SUITABLE FOR THE *ABC APPROACH*

As we have seen, careful observation of the way the child behaves is the basic starting point for putting the *ABC approach* into practice. There are several ways you can observe the child that will provide you with useful information, as long as you plan them well and carry them out methodically. Two of the most familiar types of observation, which are easy for you to do, and which are suitable for the *ABC approach*, are the *Continuous Observation* (sometimes called a Narrative Observation) and the *Focused Observation* (sometimes known as the Targeted Observation).

(For discussion of other types of observations you can use for the planning of Individual Education Plans, see Chapter 3, page 45)

The Continuous (or Narrative) Observation

The Continuous Observation is usually carried out by all the practitioners in the setting, and consists of short notes jotted down at any time during the day. The result is a running record of the child's daily progress and particular achievements. It helps to build up a longer-term picture of how the child's behaviour shows itself. Each observation note consists of a statement of what the child did, together with the related assessment statements linked into the relevant targets of the child's curriculum (Foundation stage or National Curriculum, as appropriate) and/or their Individual Education Plan. You should date and initial any observation you have made yourself, and put it into the child's profile folder.

If an observation happens to include an incident of unacceptable behaviour, it is useful to jot down a note of what was happening beforehand (the antecedent) and what happened afterwards (the consequence). Over a period of time, a pattern may appear that highlights specific elements which seem to trigger bouts of inappropriate behaviour in terms of time, person and/or place (see Chapter 3, page 48). By comparing everybody's observational jottings you could find a common thread which points to the things in the way of working with the child that need to be addressed and changed.

The Focused (or Targeted) Observation

The Focused Observation is usually carried out by just one practitioner and consists of a fixed time, usually ten or 15 minutes, where that practitioner, in a 'fly-on-the-wall' situation, records what the child does and says, in relation to the target or behaviour being addressed. Focused observations are carried out less often than continuous observations. All the staff involved with the child should decide on the number of Focused Observations to be carried out per week, half term or term, according to the child's needs. The observations are usually done at a time agreed by everybody, so that the observer can be released by the other members of staff from contact, activities or teaching. This is so he or she can concentrate completely on the task in hand and the flow of the observation will not be disrupted.

If you are doing a Focused Observation, it is important to resist the temptation to intervene if there is an incident of inappropriate behaviour during your observation session. Leave it to another practitioner to sort out the situation, and use the opportunity to note down every reaction by the child you're observing during this time. By breaking off the observation to intervene, you may well miss a crucial reaction or piece of information that could provide a vital key to the future planning of support for the child.

This is also true if you are approached by other children in the group who want to know what you're doing. From the very first observations you carry out, make it clear to all the children that you are not to be disturbed for any reason at all. You can explain to them that you are watching them all, to see what super things they're doing, and that you're writing these down in your book. It is very important not to name the target child or to make it obvious in any way that you are watching that child. This is quite easy to do by taking in other children with eye or head movements and pretending to write a word or two. But you will find that the children very soon become disinterested in what you're doing because their own activities are much more exciting.

In a Focused Observation, you should record what was happening before an observed behaviour (the antecedent), the child's observed behaviour and language (the behaviour), and what happened afterwards (the consequence).

You should then make assessment statements and link these in with the targets from the child's curriculum (Foundation stage or National Curriculum, as appropriate) and/or the targets from their Individual Education Plan.

While making a Focused Observation, you don't need to make notes on behaviours that have no bearing on the observation focus. So, for example, there is no need to write *Buster scratched his head* if the focus is Buster's ability to stand quietly in a queue.

The observation should be as objective and factual as possible, to safeguard both its accuracy and its integrity. To be objective and factual, the observation-record must show only what happened, not your opinion of what happened. For example, *Buster snatched the Lego from Annan and then thumped him on the chest* is more objective and factual than *Buster was naughty and unkind to Annan twice*. The first statement shows exactly what Buster did; the second tells us nothing except that the observer did not approve of Buster's behaviour towards Annan. 'Naughty' and 'unkind' are both subjective words, which mean different things to different people, and would tell the reader of the observation-record nothing relevant about the incident.

Because things happen fairly quickly in the 'busyness' of an early years setting, you could make notes during the observation, using key words and then write it up properly, either immediately or as soon as possible afterwards. Memories can be short or distorted when overtaken by other events in a busy setting and the professionalism of the observation must be maintained by an accurate record being written very soon after the event. Again, you should date and sign your observation report.

QUIZ TIME

Are the following statements, taken from observations, objective and factual? (Answers on page 85)

1 Soozie ran up to Jason and slapped him across the face during free choice time.

2 Brandon tore Pritpal's painting off the easel and screwed it up, before throwing it into the bin.

3 Gita was misbehaving through the whole of story time.

4 Pasqual kicked over the tower of blocks that David had made.

5 Owen stayed in the home corner and disrupted the other children's play for five minutes.

6 Walter became very aggressive towards Mina and made her very upset.

STRATEGIES FOR ENCOURAGING POSITIVE BEHAVIOUR

Once you have carried out your observations of the child and you have information about when, where and how they behave inappropriately, you are in a stronger position to start putting into place strategies that will hopefully bring about change. It may take time and the trying of different methods before you hit on the one that is most effective, but the most important thing is not to become discouraged early on and have the feeling that 'we're just not getting anywhere'.

Sometimes, children with behavioural difficulties can take quite a while before they start to show more positive behaviours. Their self-esteem may be so low that they find it hard to believe in themselves as having the ability to be 'good', and raising their self-esteem takes time.

Sometimes, they have become so used to being reprimanded that they find it difficult to handle praise or positive comments. It may be that, at first, the only way they know how to react to praise is negatively, so be prepared for this, treat the child sensitively, and make sure you do keep praising them. In time, they'll be able to take credit when it's due.

Your use of language is very important here. Try to avoid phrases such as 'Try to be a good boy, Anthony' or 'That's very naughty, Priya', since 'good' and 'naughty' are both subjective and vague, and won't mean very much to the child. Something that you consider to be 'naughty' or 'unkind' might be perfectly acceptable to the child because they're allowed to do it at home. Therefore your value judgement has no meaning for them.

If you are bringing inappropriate behaviour to the child's attention, specify what they did and why it was unacceptable. For example, 'Leave Dan's model alone, Anthony and come here to finish your own', or 'Priya, it's kinder to help Lucy with her jigsaw, so please stop throwing the pieces on the floor'.

The following are some tried and true techniques that you can have at your fingertips – you may have to work your way through several before you hit on the right one for any particular child.

- As a staff, agree to **ignore the inappropriate behaviour**. For some children, any attention, even negative attention, is a reward. If you make the mistake of becoming cross with the child and 'telling them off', you may be inadvertently rewarding the child for their undesired behaviour. This means they are more likely to repeat it. If you ignore the behaviour and make a positive effort not to become irritated by the child's behaviour, you will deprive them of the attention they're looking for. They will then realise that their behaviour doesn't get them anywhere.

- Agree to **encourage the desired behaviour** and how it is to be **positively rewarded**. It is crucial that you give immediate feedback to the child when they do something that is positive. Watch out for even the tiniest episode and praise the child straight away, using very specific language. For example, 'I'm really pleased that you helped Ahmed to tidy up the snack things, Buster. You can be very proud of yourself!' Use something concrete as a reward to show the child and everybody else in the setting that they did something positive. For example, stickers or star charts can work very effectively – they show everybody that you appreciate the child's efforts and were pleased about something specific. (If you do use stickers, they should never be removed from the child as a punishment. Also, don't let them 'outstay their welcome' – if you think that stickers are becoming devalued in the child's eyes, look for another way of recording achievements that will be as interesting and motivating for the child as the stickers were originally.)

- If unacceptable language, for example, swearing, is a problem, work with the child to **find suitable and appropriate alternatives** (which are also usually more accurate). You will be extending the child's vocabulary at the same time. For example, Buster says, 'F... off' to Jonah when Jonah asks if he can join in a game. It would be very tempting to immediately rebuke Buster and tell him not to say such rude words. But it's important to bear in mind the possibility that Buster's culture at home is different from setting's, and the word may be a normal part of his family's vocabulary – he doesn't know that you find it offensive. It would be more positive to ask Buster what he means and then talk with him to find other, more positive and specific ways of expressing what he wants to say. For example, 'No, you can't play yet Jonah – we're in the middle of this game. But you can join in the next one.'

- **Involve everybody in the planning**, where possible. This is crucial because shared information means you're more likely to have full information. For example, Buster's Mum might tell you that he has started to have temper tantrums at the supermarket checkout; the learning support assistant notices that Buster often thumps other children in the lunchtime queue and the student nursery nurse says that he refuses to help tidy up equipment after activities. Sharing the information that Buster seems to find busy times difficult to cope with, will help you to plan ways to avoid putting him into a situation that may trigger the inappropriate behaviour.

- Make sure you **have house rules that are necessary and easy to understand** for the children. You need just a few and they should be to the point. Creating a long list of rules and regulations, particularly if it is a list of 'Don'ts' will not help the children or you. They need to see the purpose of the rules before they are likely to stick to them, and they need to know exactly what's required of them through everybody (including the adults in the setting) abiding by the rules. (See Chapter 2, page 28 for a discussion of house rules.)

- Focus on and **review the layout of the setting**. It is important that you try to see the physical arrangement of the room from the child's point of view because there may be something about it that triggers the undesired behaviour. If you do identify something that needs to be changed, it is important you do this as soon as possible. Some children find large, open-plan spaces intimidating; others are frightened by the small, cosy corners that partitions can create. Tables for six or eight may put off the child who prefers to work solo or in pairs; and conversely, a cosy table for two may be just what Buster does *not* want. Perhaps shiny floor, wall and work surfaces are upsetting, or it may be that even the colour and/or the texture of the carpet in the story corner creates problems for the child. Make sure you check every possibility.

- Focus on and **review the organisation of the daily routine**: the timetable, the activities on offer and the groupings you plan. There may be aspects of your timetable that cause problems, and if you identify anything here, you should alter it. For example, Buster may find it difficult to concentrate on more demanding activities near lunchtime because he is hungry; if this is the case, then ask him to do those activities after lunch or snack time, when he's got something in his tummy to keep him going. It could be the activities themselves that trigger inappropriate behaviour. If so, it's better not to give them to Buster until he is more able to cope with the challenge they present. If there are groupings, for example one-to-one, pairs or whole-group situations, that Buster can't handle, identify which ones he finds hard to cope with and avoid putting him into that situation until he's better able to manage. Some children with emotional and/or behavioural difficulties have yet to develop social skills, and they find it extremely difficult to operate in certain group situations. Start working with the child in the type of group that they are most comfortable with, and only very gradually introduce them to other groupings.

● Focus on and **review the familiarity of the daily routine**. As we have discussed, children with behavioural difficulties need stability and security. This includes the security of knowing what is going to happen in the setting. Sometimes, a child's inappropriate behaviour is triggered by fear of and confusion about 'what's next' if this is not clear. You should try to make sure that the 'staple activities' (e.g. snack time, story time, circle time) happen at the same time every day. This will give the child confidence and security, reduce their confusion, and therefore reduce the likelihood of triggering their undesired behaviour.

● **Use pictures or symbols for the timetable** and display it at child-height. This follows on from the above point. It is extremely useful if you have the daily routine displayed on the wall in pictorial or symbolic form. The child can refer to it whenever they want to know what is going to happen next, and again, it reduces the amount of confusion felt by the child. You will find some examples of picture or symbols you can use on a timetable (Fig. 4.3) on page 92.

● As a staff, **agree on and use consistent language**. Children with behavioural difficulties need consistency, stability and routine. Part of this means everybody using the same language, so that the children know what to expect and what all the adults mean. Even something as apparently simple as referring to the same activity in different ways can cause difficulties for the child. For example, make sure you all use the same name for each working area in the setting – is it the *ICT area* or the *computer corner*? Is it the *book corner* or the *library*? Are the children going out to play in the *yard* or the *playground*? Some children are thrown into total confusion by apparently different phrases and can respond in the only way they know.

● Make sure you **have a positive and supportive relationship with the child's family**. They may well be having a tough time with the child at home, and being a 'mutual support group' will help both the parents and you, and therefore the child. It is vital that you recognise and acknowledge the important role that the parents play in the bringing up and education of their child; but it is also important that they acknowledge that you have something positive and useful to offer their child.

● To prevent episodes of unacceptable behaviour, **avoid 'trigger situations'**. This is a very important point and is not an avoidance strategy on your part. It's actually careful planning, to prevent an explosive situation developing while you're working with the child on the target behaviour. Eventually, the child will be able to manage very well in what (for them) may be a difficult situation.

- To avoid a confrontation, **offer a distraction**. The child may not have the skills to handle a situation where you and they are at loggerheads, and the predictable result is a bout of undesired behaviour. As the adult, you must take the initiative to defuse the situation. An effective way of doing this is to distract the child with something that is interesting and exciting. That way, the child will stop focusing on whatever was causing the inappropriate behaviour in the first place.

- **Offer appropriate activities.** You will be courting trouble if you ask Buster to complete an activity that challenges and overwhelms him. It is essential that you make sure the activities you offer, and the challenges they present, are within Buster's capabilities. Failure leads to frustration leads to explosion.

- Avoid overload and **break down activities into small steps**. It is important that you offer activities in 'bite-size' pieces that the child has the skills to manage. As they make progress, you can increase the steps and make the challenge a little bigger. Sometimes, the child has a very short concentration span and/or a low level of interest, so they must experience instant success if they are not to become immediately frustrated. Let them begin their activity from a point at which they can achieve success or reward, and move on from there. Monitor their progress carefully and as soon as they are struggling to achieve, reduce the steps a bit, so helping to avoid an explosion of inappropriate behaviour caused by frustration and failure.

- Before you speak, **attract the child's attention**. Children with behavioural difficulties may not always realise that instructions or comments you make to a group are also for them as individuals. It is important that you have the child's attention before beginning to speak. You can start your sentence by saying the child's name and gaining eye contact before continuing. If you prefer to use several names, to avoid singling out any particular child, make sure you always say that child's name first, and use a maximum of three names. You can also gently touch the child on the shoulder, encouraging them to focus on you. But – do this only if the child will tolerate being touched, and if you are comfortable doing it, in relation to health and safety, and/or child protection issues. Use your professional judgement here.

- Help to reduce confusion and **warn of activity changes**. As we have seen, the child needs stability and security, and it is crucial that you signal a change of activity beforehand. You can use an egg timer as a prompt. For example, start the timer and say, 'When the sand runs out, it will be time to clear up and have our story.' Watching the sand run through the glass gives the child a concrete way of marking the change in activities.

- **Anticipate dangerous situations.** For example, if the child has a habit of running out of the playground, make sure a safety lock is fitted on the gate; if they like to poke straws into electric sockets, put in safety blanking plates; if they're less than sensible with scissors, keep the scissors out of reach and let the child use them appropriately under supervision.

- To avoid confusion, **give clear instructions**, repeating them if necessary. Some children find it very hard to take instructions on board and you may need to repeat them several times. Make sure you're facing the child full on when you're giving them instructions.

- **Give instructions in small steps.** Sometimes a child finds difficulty in managing a multiple instruction, so you should reduce it to the number of elements that they can manage. For example, Buster may find it hard to follow 'OK everybody, put away your toys, put your coats on and go outside to play'. It's likely that he will retain either 'Put away your toys' (the first element) or 'Go outside to play' (the last element), and will seem to be defiant because he tidied up his toys and then just stood there, or because he rushed straight outside without tidying up or putting on his coat. Give your instructions in single elements, or two at the most: (i) 'OK, Buster, tidy away your toys'; (ii) 'Good boy, now put your coat on'; (iii) 'OK – you can go out to play now. Enjoy your playtime!'

- **Have a quiet area available.** This is worth a king's fortune if your setting can afford the space. It is *crucial* that you promote the quiet area as somewhere pleasant and positive, where the child is free to go if they want to work quietly, read or play. Encourage them to go there if they need to come away from an explosive or frustrating situation for a few moments to calm down. Let them go there with their key practitioner to talk about their feelings and so on. The quiet area must *never* be used as a punishment, or as a place for 'time out', or as a 'sin bin'.

- Use free play sessions to **break up periods of structured activity.** Some children's concentration span is short and they may find it difficult to stay on task, even for relatively short periods of time. If you are aware of this, then intersperse the structured activities with a few minutes of an activity of the child's choice. This is not pampering the child, but helping to avoid a situation where they may feel frustrated at being forced to stay on task for longer than they can manage, with unacceptable behaviour being the result. If appropriate, you can have one of the IEP targets as *To increase Buster's concentration span to 30 seconds / two minutes / five minutes* and so on as appropriate.

CASE STUDIES

You might like to consider the following questions for each of these case studies. There are no 'right' or 'wrong' answers, but you should take into account all the information about each child while deciding how to plan for them. You will find some suggestions at the end of the chapter:

1 What may be triggering the child's inappropriate behaviour(s)?

2 Does the existing management strategy seem to be effective?

3 What targets would you choose for the child to work towards?

4 What are the child's positive points and strengths?

5 What effective strategies would you adopt to help the child achieve their target(s)?

CASE STUDY A: Philip, 4 years

Philip was diagnosed with an autistic spectrum disorder at 3 years and he attends mornings only at his local nursery school. When he is not allowed to do what he wants, which is usually doing jigsaws that he has an obsession about, he will have a severe temper tantrum. He screams and throws across the room anything small that's near to hand. His tantrum subsides if he is given his own way. Philip has very little verbal communication and he is unable to work to a routine. He never interacts with the other children or joins in with their play, preferring to do his jigsaws alone.

Existing management strategies
When Philip has a tantrum either he is allowed to get on with a jigsaw, or one of the practitioners will put him into the quiet area of the room by himself and leave him there. His tantrum eventually subsides and he moans to himself until a practitioner brings him out.

CASE STUDY B: Clara, 3 years

Clara has limited language skills, both expressive and receptive, and she has severe behavioural difficulties. She was expelled from her playgroup because of her behaviour and now goes to her local day nursery four mornings a week. When she arrives for the start of a session, she tries to destroy any toys or games that are out. She runs wildly around the room and is difficult to control. She will kick or bite adults or children for no apparent reason.

Existing management strategies
The practitioners often tell Clara off and warn her that she must be a good girl and behave properly towards other people. Her key worker will take her into the book corner when she has tried to bite or kick, and stays with her, sharing books together, until she calms down.

CASE STUDY C: Theo, 5 years

Theo was diagnosed as having ADHD when he was 4 years old. He attends his local mainstream school, in the Reception class with 22 other children, and he has a part-time Learning Support Assistant. At the moment, he is taking the drug Ritalin. When the class has sessions in the hall, Theo stands screaming. His maximum concentration span is about 50 seconds. He communicates effectively with his LSA during calm periods. He finds difficulty in remembering the classroom timetable and he runs around wildly when activities change.

Existing management strategies
When he is having a screaming session, Theo's LSA takes him into the school library to look at books and talk to him until he's quiet, which he quite enjoys. When he begins to run around the classroom, the LSA takes him out into the playground until she considers he is behaving properly.

CASE STUDY D: Ravi, 4 years

Until recently, Ravi, who is an only child, attended his local nursery on a part-time basis (afternoons only), but he's now increasing to full time before his transfer to primary school. He's a bright child and seems to enjoy doing the activities on offer, usually completing them very quickly. He prefers to play with one or two children and always wants to direct the game. He will pinch or hit the other children if they won't do as he tells them, ordering them to go away from the game, saying, 'I'm not allowing you to play my game'. Ravi is doing this more often now, and on occasion he pinches or hits another child for no apparent reason, sometimes just doing it as he passes them.

Existing management strategies
When Ravi pinches or hits a child during a game, the practitioner takes him away and gives him a solitary activity to do, telling him if he can't 'play nicely' then he has to do some work. She usually gives him a photocopiable sheet to complete, and he will sit quietly for quite a long time doing the 'work' he has been set. If he hits or pinches another child without apparent provocation, she deprives him of his free choice at 'Choose Time' and involves him in an adult-led activity while the others are doing their unstructured activities. This is on a one-to-one basis and he will stay on task for long periods of time.

SUMMARY

In this chapter we explored strategies for both reducing inappropriate behaviour and encouraging positive behaviour by

- examining the *ABC approach* to behaviour management;

- exploring some ways of observing and identifying inappropriate behaviour;

- suggesting positive and effective interventions, including some general principles behind managing challenging behaviour in the setting, and also some more specific strategies;

- using case studies as a basis for exploring ways of planning for specific children.

Answers to Quiz time (page 77)

1 Yes. The statement tells us exactly what Soozie did.

2 Yes. We know what Brandon's behaviour consisted of from the statement.

3 Mostly no. We have no idea what Gita was doing. 'Misbehaving' tells us nothing beyond the notion that the observer disapproved of Gita's behaviour. There is some factual information since we know when she was behaving inappropriately, but we don't know what she did.

4 Yes. Pasqual's actions are described factually.

5 Mostly no. We have the factual information that tells us where and for how long the inappropriate behaviour took place, but the term 'disrupted' doesn't give us any indication of what Owen was doing.

6 No. 'Aggressive' is a subjective word in this context and doesn't tell us what exactly Walter was doing to Mina. Neither do we know what Mina's reaction is, since 'very upset' is a vague description which gives little useful information.

SOME SUGGESTED RESPONSES TO THE QUESTIONS ABOUT THE CASE STUDIES:

Case study A: Philip

1 What may be triggering the child's inappropriate behaviour(s)?

- There is a reduction in the demands made of him by others and he is removed from the stressful situation – this makes him feel more comfortable.

- His ability to communicate his needs and desires is limited.

- He is confused about the routine and activities in the setting.

2 Does the existing management strategy seem to be effective?

- Yes for the adults, who seem to want Philip out of the way for a quiet life.

- No for Philip – from his moaning, we know he is still distressed; his social and educational needs are not being supported; his personal development is not being encouraged.

3 What targets would you choose for the child to work towards?

- Working with other children and adults to develop his social skills.

- Helping him to learn the daily routine of the setting.

- Reduction of undesired behaviours such as throwing equipment and screaming.

- Development of his communication skills

4 What are the child's positive points and strengths?

- He is good at doing jigsaws. The practitioners can use this skill as a starting point for his IEP targets.

- He will eventually calm down if he is allowed his own way. The practitioners can turn this into a 'positive' starting point.

5 What effective strategies would you adopt to help the child achieve their target(s)?

- Decide on a positive approach by the practitioners, i.e. they should not 'banish' Philip until they are ready to bring him out. This positive approach should be used consistently by everybody.

- Agree to identify and reward any positive behaviour Philip displays.

- Put up a picture/symbol timetable so Philip can easily see what will be happening at each session of the day.

- Use Philip's love of jigsaws as a starting point to work on one-to-one, then gradually introduce more children until he can work in pairs and then small groups.

- Discuss with Philip's parents and the other practitioners the possibility of involving specialist agencies for advice on behaviour management.

● Case study B: Clara

1 What may be triggering the child's inappropriate behaviour(s)?

- Clara may be totally overwhelmed by the 'busyness' of the room.

- She may be very confused about the routine, not knowing what is supposed to be happening when.

- She may feel frustrated because of her limited communication skills which prevent her from expressing her needs and wants.

2 Does the existing management strategy seem to be effective?

- Yes, if calming Clara down is the intention, but she may calm down even without the strategy.
- No, if the intention is to help Clara make sense of what's going on around her, since she clearly has no idea of exactly what's expected of her. Phrases such as 'Be a good girl' and 'Behave properly' mean very little to her because they are not specific enough.

3 What targets would you choose for the child to work towards?

- Clara's language and communication skills.
- Helping her to understand the setting's daily routine.
- Helping her to develop positive behaviour skills, being specific about what she should be doing and what is not going to be tolerated.
- Helping her to develop her social skills.

4 What are the child's positive points and strengths?

- Clara is interested in books and enjoys looking at them.
- She has well-developed gross motor skills – she can run and kick well. This could be used as a starting point for her programme.

5 What effective strategies would you adopt to help the child achieve their target(s)?

- The staff could make a quiet and distraction-free area for Clara to work in.
- Put up a picture/symbol timetable showing the daily routine.
- Give Clara specific and positive guidelines for behaviour that is expected of her.
- Use her running and kicking skills to encourage activities and games with other children.

Case study C: Theo

1 What may be triggering the child's inappropriate behaviour(s)?

- Theo actually achieves something he finds pleasurable when he behaves inappropriately.
- He may have a sense of insecurity in large open areas such as the hall.
- He may feel insecure in group work or situations with other children close by.
- He has no ability to follow the daily routine and this may result in confusion about what's going on around him.
- The drug (Ritalin) may be having a detrimental affect.

2 Does the existing management strategy seem to be effective?

- Yes, if the objective is a series of breaks away from Theo for the practitioner.
- No, if Theo's overall development is to make any headway.

3 What targets would you choose for the child to work towards?

- Theo needs to work on social interactions and skills.
- He needs support in learning to control his inappropriate behaviour.
- Helping him to understand the daily routine of the classroom.
- Helping him to increase his concentration span.

4 What are the child's positive points and strengths?

- Theo's communication skills are well developed.
- He eventually calms down after a bout of screaming or inappropriate behaviour.
- He enjoys looking at books.

5 What effective strategies would you adopt to help the child achieve their target(s)?

- Put up the timetable in picture or symbol form and help him to refer to it regularly throughout the day.
- Use his interest in books as a starting point for working towards his chosen targets.
- When the class goes in for hall sessions, his LSA could take Theo into the hall after the other children have gone in and have settled down.

Case study D: Ravi

1 What may be triggering the child's inappropriate behaviour(s)?

- Ravi may find difficulty sharing with other children. As a singleton, he won't have had the experience of the 'give and take' of living with siblings.
- He may be finding full time sessions tiring, being used to mornings only for quite some time.
- He may not be challenged enough. As a bright child who finishes his activities quickly, he could be finding the curriculum on offer a bit easy. He could be bored.
- He may be attention seeking.

2 Does the existing management strategy seem to be effective?

- No. Ravi's inappropriate behaviour seems to be increasing, and the strategies don't help him to learn how to turn-take or to share.

3 What targets would you choose for the child to work towards?

- Sharing and turn-taking.
- Playing and working in groups.
- More challenging targets in the areas where he seems to be 'understretched'.

4 What are the child's positive points and strengths?

- Ravi has a high achievement level.
- His concentration span is very good.
- He has some leadership skills that could be channelled in a positive direction.

5 What effective strategies would you adopt to help the child achieve their target(s)?

- A reduction of activities for only one or two children and a gradual increase of involvement with group play and activities.
- Observe, assess and identify the specific areas of Ravi's achievement and plan more challenging activities to 'stretch' him appropriately and prevent him from becoming bored.
- A positive behaviour plan which aims to reduce Ravi's episodes of pinching or hitting other children. Ravi must be involved in both the planning and the record keeping of the programme. With specific criteria in terms of time spans and expected behaviour, the plan will help Ravi to increase his positive behaviour.
- Use more appropriate methods of sanction for Ravi's unacceptable behaviour. To make a marked distinction between 'work' and 'play', and then use 'work' as a sanction (i.e. the photocopiable worksheets) establishes in Ravi's mind a perception of a difference between the two, which goes against the philosophy of the Foundation stage curriculum.
- Ask Ravi's parents for their input to the plan and support by continuing it at home by, for example, rewarding him appropriately when he brings home a 'Positive Behaviour Certificate'.

Figure 4.1 An example of a completed *ABC approach* observation form

Child's name and d.o.b.: Buster Clayton; 13.2.00 Observer's name: Anne Jones	Date and time of observation: 09.15 – 11.00 15.2.2004	Focus of observation/area of learning: Personal, social and emotional development
Antecedents: what led up to the behaviour?	Behaviour: what exactly did the child do?	Consequences: what happened afterwards?
9.15 Children sitting for registration and allocation of activities. Manjit asked Buster to sit quietly during register time.	Buster shouted out each child's name as they answered the register and hit the child beside him.	Buster left the group and ran towards the computer. He refused to rejoin the group when Manjit asked him to come back.
10.30 Children doing a variety of structured activities. Manjit had prepared four for Buster.	Buster ran around the room and refused to do his activities. He destroyed other children's models, painting and sand play.	He told Manjit to 'F... off' and went to the computer corner. He sat under the computer table.
11.00 Children having snack.	Buster threw his juice down the sink and his biscuit on the floor.	I took him to the quiet corner and helped him to calm down. He apologised to Manjit for swearing and to the other children for spoiling their games.

ABC approach observation form

Child's name and d.o.b.: Observer's name:	Date and time of observation:	Focus of observation/area of learning:
Antecedents: what led up to the behaviour?	Behaviour: what exactly did the child do?	Consequences: what happened afterwards?

Figure 4.2   **Some symbols that can be used for a pictorial timetable**

Glossary of some educational acronyms

ADD	Attention Deficit Disorder
ADHD	Attention Deficit Hyperactive Disorder
BSS	Behaviour Support Service
CPS	Child Psychology Service
DfES	Department for Education and Skills
DES	Department of Education and Science
DOE	Director of Education
EBD	Emotional and Behavioural Difficulties
EP	Educational Psychologist (may also be known as Ed. Psych.)
EPS	Educational Psychology Service
EYBSS	Early Years Behaviour Support Service
EYSSS	Early Years Sensory Support Service
EYDCP	Early Years Development and Childcare Partnership
EYLSS	Early Years Learning Support Service
GP	General Practitioner
HIS	Hearing Impairment Service
HISS	Hearing Impairment Support Service
HIV	Human Immunodeficiency Virus
HV	Health Visitor
IAP	Individual Action Programme
IEP	Individual Education Plan
IL	Interactive Learning
IPSS	Independent Parental Support Service
LD	Learning Difficulties
LEA	Local Education Authority
LSA	Learning Support Assistant
LSS	Learning Support Service
MLD	Mild or Moderate Learning Difficulties

PA	Plan of Action
PP	Play plan
PSS	Parental Support Service
SEASS	Special Educational Advisory and Support Service
SEN	Special Educational Needs
SENCO	Special Educational Needs Coordinator
SISS	Sensory Impairment Support Service
SLD	Specific Learning Difficulties/Speech and Language Difficulties/ Severe Learning Difficulties
VIS	Visual Impairment Service
VISS	Visual Impairment Support Service

Figure 1   **Acronym crossword solution**

1. E	Y	D	C	2. P		3. D	
B				S		F	
D		4. L	5. S	S		6. E	P
	7. L		E			S	
	8. S	9. E	N	C	O		
10. I	A	P				11. I	12. L
E		13. S	I	S	S		E
14. P	P					15. P	A

Further reading

Autism in the Early Years, Val Cumine, Julia Leach and Gill Stevenson (David Fulton Publishers, 2000).

Special Educational Needs Code of Practice (DfES, 2001).

SEN Toolkit (DfES, 2001).

All Together, How to create inclusive services for disabled children and their families, M. Dickins and J. Denziloe (National Children's Bureau 2003, 1st edn. National Early Years Network, 1998).

Special needs in early years settings, a practitioner's guide, Collette Drifte (David Fulton Publishers, 2002).

Early learning goals and children with special needs, Collette Drifte (David Fulton Publishers, 2002).

Handbook for Pre-School SEN Provision: The SEN Code of Practice in relation to the early years, Collette Drifte (David Fulton Publishers, 2003).

Effective IEPs through Circle Time: practical solutions to writing Individual Education Plans for children with emotional and behavioural difficulties, Margaret Goldthorpe (LDA, 2001, 1st edn. 1998).

Observation and record keeping, Ann Henderson (Pre-school Learning Alliance, 1994).

Behaviour in Pre-school Groups, Ann Henderson (Pre-school Learning Alliance, 1995).

Right from the Start: Effective planning and assessment in the early years, Vicky Hutchin (Hodder & Stoughton, 1999).

Developing Individual Behaviour Plans in the Early Years, Hannah Mortimer (NASEN, 2000).

Taking Part, Hannah Mortimer (QEd, 2000).

Behavioural and emotional Difficulties, Dr Hannah Mortimer (Scholastic, 2002).

Supporting Children with AD/HD and Attention Difficulties in the Early Years, Dr Hannah Mortimer (QEd, 2002).

Working Towards a Whole School Policy on Self-Esteem and Positive Behaviour, Jenny Mosley (Positive Press, 2001).

Understanding Children's Challenging Behaviour, Penny Mukherji (Nelson Thornes, 2001).

Supporting Special Needs, Understanding Inclusion in the Early Years, Penny Tassoni (Heinemann, 2003).

Special Needs and Early Years, a practitioner's guide, Kate Wall (Paul Chapman Publishing, 2003).

Create Happier Lunchtimes: Ideas for Primary Midday Supervisors, Wiltshire County Council (WEST, 2001, 1st edn. 1997).

Index